P9-BZT-938

ON THE RADIO

ON THE RADIO
with Harden and Weaver

FRANK HARDEN
AND
JACKSON WEAVER
WITH
ED MEYER

William Morrow and Company
New York 1983

Grateful acknowledgment is made for permission to quote from "Pilot of the Airwaves," words and music by Charlie Dore, copyright © 1979, 1980 by Ackee Music, Inc. (ASCAP). All rights reserved. Used by permission.

Library of Congress Cataloging in Publication Data

Harden, Frank.
On the radio.

Includes index.
1. Harden, Frank. 2. Weaver, Jackson. 3. Radio broadcasters—Washington (D.C.)—Biography. I. Weaver, Jackson. II. Meyer, Ed. III. Title.
PN1991.4.A2H37 1983 791.44'092'2[B] 83-7980
ISBN 0-688-02032-1

Printed in the United States of America

First Edition

1 2 3 4 5 6 7 8 9 10

BOOK DESIGN BY MARIA EPES

FOREWORD

A Tough Act to Follow...

Washington, D.C., is a tough act to follow. We've had some pretty big names here over the years. For instance, how do you follow Washington, Jefferson, Lincoln, Roosevelt, Give-'em-hell Harry, and—lord knows—Watergate?

Most people tend to think of politics when they think of Washington, D.C., and rightly so. Most if not all of the big-name politicos have played Washington at one time or another. It is also logical that many big news names either played here or even cut their journalistic teeth in this city. Morgan Beatty, Fulton Lewis, Jr., on radio and in more recent times, David Brinkley, Roger Mudd and the venerable Walter Cronkite are all Washington, D.C., alums. But did you ever stop to think how many really honest-to-goodness show business stars got their start right here in the nation's capital? They are legendary and their numbers are formidable. For example, there's Kate Smith, Helen Hayes, Al Jolson, The Muppets, Jimmy Dean, Roberta Flack, Mama Cass, Goldie Hawn, Shirley MacLaine, and of course the granddaddy of them all, Arthur Godfrey . . . a procession of superstars.

One reason I have always felt Washington is a good proving ground for talent, other than political, is the fact that most everybody who lives there comes from someplace else. The old line "Will it play in Peoria?" is applicable here. If you are a hit in Washington . . . in other words if you can be successful I believe you can make it in show business anywhere. You are playing to a cross-section of the entire country when you play in the nation's capital.

It was September 1950 when I first met the dashing duo Frank Harden and Jackson Weaver. I had just started my job as an NBC page at WRC Radio in the Trans-Lux Building at Fourteenth Street and New York Avenue. Radio buffs may recall the Red and the Blue Networks, both owned by RCA. NBC was the Red Network, and the present-day ABC was the Blue Network. Even though ABC had split from RCA back in the forties, they were both in the same building. I was attending American University at the time, and WMAL-TV's transmitter was located on the campus. We were doing one of those early-day TV singing and dancing specials. Frank and Jack—even though their radio show was not on the air at that time—were hosts. The only thing I remember about that entire experience was that Jackson Weaver was supposed to be drinking a cup of tea. Well, the prop man (obviously a friend of Jackson's) substituted booze for the tea and all of us kids thought this was really great stuff. One sip and Jackson's false beard came unglued! Both men were always terrific announcers and successful talents in their own right before they became a radio team, a factor that never hurt a team relationship. Frank was the announcer for the Edward P. Morgan news show on ABC; Jack was the announcer for the U.S. Navy Band hour on ABC; and—perhaps his greatest role of all times—Jack was the voice of Smokey the Bear for the Park Service.

Thirty-two years later (and older), here I am writing the foreword for their book, and I honestly believe there has never been a more successful radio team in the industry. Other radio station managements have sent people to study their show and format to try to figure out how a morning

ACKNOWLEDGMENTS

Beyond those persons mentioned in the text, the authors wish to give recognition to others who have been of invaluable assistance in the preparation of this book.

To Janice Iacona, who saw to it that deadlines were met and for her liaison with the publishers. To Andy Ockershausen whose memory for dates and occasions far exceeded ours. To broadcast engineers Donna Harrell, Vickie Hill, Ed Painter and Gail Granata for covering what would have been dead spots on the air while we digressed about the book. To Barbara Meyer for turning barely legible scribblings into typescript. And to Elsie Weaver and Berit Harden for inordinate amounts of patience and support.

radio team can stay number one for twenty-five years on a 5,000-watt station in a sophisticated city like Washington, D.C. They talk 80 percent of the program time, and when they do play music, it's usually a Joe "Fingers" Carr tune like "Yes, Sir, That's My Baby," while the other forty stations in the market are beating each other's brains out for the ratings, playing The Grateful Dead, and with a minimum of chatter. On paper or in format it just shouldn't work in modern radio, but it has and it does for one, or should I say two, simple reasons: Harden and Weaver. They are successful because they are themselves—they are real and honest with each other and their audience. They love what they do and have a good time doing it, and the audience shares in this fun. They are dedicated to public service and have been very active in the community for all the time they have been on the air. Perhaps the most important single factor—the GIFT I call it—is that they were made for each other and found each other. They are not the result of Central Casting or some consulting firm; their Marriage was made in Heaven. A team like Harden and Weaver cannot be created, it has to happen. The audience senses this and responds to it.

I have said more than enough. Let them speak for themselves through the following pages. I love them both very much and wish them continued success; and since they say confession is good for the soul, I hereby reveal, Jackson, that it was I who substituted the booze for the tea back in 1950.

WILLARD H. SCOTT

Delaplane, Virginia

ACKNOWLEDGMENTS

Beyond those persons mentioned in the text, the authors wish to give recognition to others who have been of invaluable assistance in the preparation of this book.

To Janice Iacona, who saw to it that deadlines were met and for her liaison with the publishers. To Andy Ockershausen whose memory for dates and occasions far exceeded ours. To broadcast engineers Donna Harrell, Vickie Hill, Ed Painter and Gail Granata for covering what would have been dead spots on the air while we digressed about the book. To Barbara Meyer for turning barely legible scribblings into typescript. And to Elsie Weaver and Berit Harden for inordinate amounts of patience and support.

radio team can stay number one for twenty-five years on a 5,000-watt station in a sophisticated city like Washington, D.C. They talk 80 percent of the program time, and when they do play music, it's usually a Joe "Fingers" Carr tune like "Yes, Sir, That's My Baby," while the other forty stations in the market are beating each other's brains out for the ratings, playing The Grateful Dead, and with a minimum of chatter. On paper or in format it just shouldn't work in modern radio, but it has and it does for one, or should I say two, simple reasons: Harden and Weaver. They are successful because they are themselves—they are real and honest with each other and their audience. They love what they do and have a good time doing it, and the audience shares in this fun. They are dedicated to public service and have been very active in the community for all the time they have been on the air. Perhaps the most important single factor—the GIFT I call it—is that they were made for each other and found each other. They are not the result of Central Casting or some consulting firm; their Marriage was made in Heaven. A team like Harden and Weaver cannot be created, it has to happen. The audience senses this and responds to it.

I have said more than enough. Let them speak for themselves through the following pages. I love them both very much and wish them continued success; and since they say confession is good for the soul, I hereby reveal, Jackson, that it was I who substituted the booze for the tea back in 1950.

WILLARD H. SCOTT

Delaplane, Virginia

". . . I've been listenin' to your show on the radio . . . and you seem like a friend to me."

—*"Pilot of the Airwaves"*
Music and lyrics by Charlie Dore

HARDEN AND WEAVER GALLERY

FRANK (on phone): Bosco, what are you doing in Tampa? You're supposed to be covering the Super Bowl in Pontiac, Michigan.

BOSCO: There was some kind of mix-up. But look here, I'm running short of money. There's this young girl I ran into—really sweet—working her way through college, and we're having breakfast now and . . .

FRANK: Bosco, we have a very bad connection, so . . .

BOSCO: I mean the lady has had around sixteen champagne cocktails, and I'm gonna need some more . . .

FRANK: Bosco, I'm having a devil of a time hearing this, so . . .

BOSCO: DON'T HANG UP! I'm really in trouble because . . .

FRANK: Talk to you later, Bosco . . .

BOSCO: Listen now, you gotta help me out. I mean this girl . . .
(Click)

Jackson: Sign On

George Weaver was a lumberjack who had a sharp ax and a big drinking problem. That combination alone would have tended to make him a rather independent fellow. He wasn't someone you were apt to pick a fight with over just any old thing. In other words, George was a pretty rough character—at least that's the story. All of that was before I knew him as my grandfather. By that time he had put down the ax and the bottle, dumped lumberjacking and become a carpenter. That's what he did from then on, and he was still doing it till the day he died when he was in his eighties.

You might say George Weaver exercised a substantial influence on my life. We all lived together in Buffalo, New York, in a house on Milford Street—my grandfather, my grandmother, my mother and father, two brothers and two sisters. My grandfather was what I guess people today would call "macho." He tried to teach me about how you had to make your own breaks in life—the old "pull yourself up by your bootstraps" routine. If I picked up some toughness from him, I got the other side of the coin from my grandmother, Priscilla. She was very loving and concentrated on the tender things of life. That was fine by me. There was room for both in a young lad's life.

My father—John Weaver—was a railroad engineer on the

old Pennsylvania Railroad, and he had the run between Oil City, Pennsylvania, and Buffalo. He was born in Oil City and my mother was born in Buffalo. Obviously he stopped in Buffalo long enough to marry her and set this whole thing in motion.

Except for my grandparents I'm not very familiar with the family tree. My Weaver ancestors came here from Germany. One of them—Johan Webar—came across in a sailing ship and landed in what is now Philadelphia. Somewhere along the way, Webar became Weaver; and from Philadelphia the family moved westward in Pennsylvania.

We all ended up in that two-family house in Buffalo—with my grandparents upstairs and the rest of us on the first floor. It was the happiest of arrangements. I can't remember anything that disturbed my life at all in those early years.

From the very beginning I loved boats and the sea. Buffalo was a great port—they called it the "Queen City of the Lakes"—and Lake Erie was my private property. It fascinated me. All the shipping came in from as far west as Duluth, Minnesota. Great shiploads of wheat would be transported either on the railroads or by barge on the Erie Canal. I would hang around the waterfront docks, and once in a while I would be allowed aboard a ship. At fourteen, I was simply waiting to be old enough to apply to the Merchant Marine Academy in Kings Point, New York. I would then become an officer in the merchant service and spend the rest of my life aboard those great ships.

On occasion I rode on the *Americana* and the *Canadiana* between Buffalo and Crystal Beach, Canada. I spent so much time on these ships the captains and engineers all knew me and would let me into the engine rooms. I'd spend the whole day riding back and forth; to me that was the best life in the world.

Lake Erie was almost a ninety-minute walk from my house and I'd practically worn a path. One day—I guess I was about twelve—a friend and I rented a rowboat and headed for the Alhambra dance hall at Woodlawn Beach—about fifteen miles away. We got there in pretty good time and spent the day swimming and fooling around, and before we stopped to think about it the sun was going down. We headed back, but we weren't out very long before it got really dark. We could see some lights along the shore, but the lake itself was pitch black.

Here we were rowing this little boat for all we were worth, and I don't know what worried us more, the lake or what was awaiting us when we got home. Finally we came up to the Lackawanna Steel Plant. We could see the huge carloads of white-hot slag being poured down into the lake, and we could hear the hiss of steam as they hit the water. At least this was something familiar—we knew pretty much where we were—but we were still quite a distance from home. Finally we came to the breakwater, and as we were rowing through it I heard a high whine like a dynamo. I asked my friend, "Do you hear something?" He answered, "Yeah—what the heck is it?" We stopped rowing in the darkness and looked all around. Then we saw it—a huge lake freighter—about twenty feet away. It seemed like some monster of the deep—about five hundred feet long, towering above us by six or seven stories. Apparently it had moved in quietly waiting for a tugboat escort and was sitting there almost dead in the water. We were really scared to death. Here we were out there with no lights or navigational warning system of any kind and on a collision course with a huge freighter!

It was about then that the tug came along and heard our shouts, and turned a big spotlight on us. The people aboard called us every name in the book—some words I've never heard since. Anyhow we made it back to shore, and I suppose I learned a few lessons from that ill-conceived voyage. But it didn't diminish my love for boats and the sea. Soon, however, another interest was to compete for my time and thoughts.

Jackson: Shut Up and Start Talking

Blame it all on Adelbert—Adelbert Sprague. He was one of my junior high school teachers who also ran the drama department and the debating team. I acted in the plays and was on the debating team, and it wasn't long before he was bugging me to audition for radio dramas at a local radio station. I was only fourteen, but I had a natural talent for acting and a very good ear for dialects. I could reproduce someone's accent almost immediately after hearing it. Buffalo was a melting pot, so there was no shortage of dialects to copy. Many of the kids in my school spoke foreign languages at home, and I would come in contact with them that way. I began building up a repertoire of dialect stories simply to entertain my brothers and sisters and friends. I did it strictly for amusement—it never occurred to me that there would be any use down the line for this sort of thing, or that there was a demand for it in a professional way. But apparently it had occurred to Adelbert Sprague. My personality also lent itself to acting. I was very outgoing—my whole family was that way. So when Adelbert finally convinced me to take the plunge, I put together some material. I wrote eight monologues—all of them, naturally, in different dialects. I figured that had to impress somebody. I got a lot of help in the preparation from a neighbor named Ed Kelly who lived across the street. Ed was an old newspaperman. He was partially paralyzed and would sit out on his porch on a rocking chair, and I spent a great deal of time talking with him. He helped me write the material and also encouraged me. I had needed some convincing, which he provided and gave me the feeling that I wasn't just wasting a lot of time.

I studied those monologues and carried them with me to the audition Adelbert had arranged for me at station WKBW in the Rand Building in Buffalo. It was 1934—not the best of times for teenage job seekers. For purposes of morale, I took my twelve-year-old brother, Richard, with me.

Fred Dampier, the head of radio drama programming, auditioned me. Afterward he offered me a job on a free-lance basis. He would use me when he had a part for me. I was paid $2.50 per program—including the rehearsal time. Over the next four years I got an increasing number of parts and became more and more fascinated by the radio business. You have to remember that radio was a glamorous profession in those pre-TV days of the 1930s, and this was pretty heady stuff for a teenager. I started out in small parts, but it was my knack for dialects that really opened things up for me. They could plug me in just about anywhere for a change of pace. Other people could play one or two types—I could do not only accents but voice changes, too. The opportunities became limitless. I was flying high—cutting classes at school in the afternoon when there was a radio show to do. Before long, I was a member of the WBEN Players—doing shows for WBEN as well as for WKBW.

Lake Erie was still out there. But it was not beckoning so strongly now. I was too caught up in this new, exciting business, so much so that I suddenly dropped out of high school in my second year. I've always felt that was one of my big mistakes. It wasn't a case of either radio or school—I could have managed both. I guess I got disenchanted with going to classes. I'd been an average student, no world beater, but I wasn't having any trouble, I simply up and quit. I suppose I was already setting my sights on becoming a big-time radio announcer and nothing else mattered. Whatever the reason, it was not a good one.

With school out of the way, I was working at as many as four radio stations on a free-lance basis, and amassing the sum of $20 a week. I was paying board at home and buying my own clothes and feeling pretty big-time. The more I worked, the more parts seemed to come my way. I was eating it up—running from station to station. Everything was coming up roses. I began to think in terms of someday dropping this drama stuff, joining those hotshot announcers on the networks in New York City and making those big dollars. Of course, I hadn't done any announcing yet, but that didn't bother me. Any kid, I thought, who could break into radio by age fourteen should be hot stuff by the time he's eighteen. I knew I would have to start announcing at a small station, and finally got my chance at WBNY in Buffalo.

I was eighteen years old when I reported for an audition to WBNY, a little station on the second floor of a building at Mohawk and Main streets. The station was part of the New York State Network, a regional network. But it was large enough for me. When I was told I had passed the audition and would be making $15 a week, it was one of the happiest moments of my life. I went home—swung my mother around the room hollering, "I'm a radio announcer! I'm a radio announcer!" You'd have thought I'd just graduated from medical school!

At WBNY I began the process of learning everything I could about the business. Small stations are perfect for this because you do a little bit of everything. You learn the entire business, not just one segment of it as you are apt to do if you join a large station early in your career. You follow the progress of a radio program from the beginning—from the sale of the spot announcement, the writing of the copy, getting it on the log to integrating it into the program and finally airing it. You learn radio's traffic system and enough engineering to be able to operate the controls that keep the program on the air.

But while the small station is an excellent training ground, it is only a step along the way for the ambitious. A little more money soon beckons elsewhere. For me, it was Manitowoc, Wisconsin. I received a telegram from a friend who was working at WOMT in Manitowoc and pulling down $26 a week, almost double my salary. Not only that, he said there was a job opening and he could get me on as a staff announcer. My friend also extolled the virtues of this lovely little town on Lake Michigan—being careful not to tell me about the weather, which made Buffalo seem like Miami Beach.

I talked it over with my folks and decided to take the job. No audition. My friend arranged everything. This was my first venture away from home. I had to take a train to Chicago and change there for Manitowoc. By the time the train reached Sheboygan, I was wondering when the Indians were going to attack. It was all pretty exciting—and I was looking forward to this second step on the way to the big time in New York, although I had a funny feeling I was heading in the wrong direction. Being pretty much of a city fella, I was wearing a Chesterfield coat, a Homburg hat and pigskin gloves, when I stepped off the train, and must have looked to the locals like some kind of medicine show come to town. Here they were in their brown corduroys, high boots, mackinaws and hats pulled down over their ears, smoking their pipes, looking at me with a great deal of curiosity as if to say, "We'd better keep an eye on this dude."

I rented a room over a saloon and settled in. It was 1939. Europe was already beginning to explode. But in Manitowoc,

Wisconsin, my only concern was the weather. I was going to work when the temperature was 16 degrees below zero. I mean, Buffalo is no place for thin blood, but this place was ridiculous.

The radio station was a real piece of work. It was a 100-watter—that's so small it's hardly worth it. Generally if the transmitters are inside the radio station, they are placed in racks, all neat and orderly. Ours was sitting out in the middle of the floor. Each piece was wired up to the next, and there were lights flashing all over the place. I'm not sure how we ever got on the air. I'm not sure we always *were!*

We had only two announcers, plus a lady who was the program director and filled in as a part-time announcer. There were six people on the staff. Since we had to have a day off, the station went off the air one day a week. The studio was used that day for polka dances. I was the morning man—with sign-on at sunup—and the on-the-air shift would end at noon. There was an engineer, so we didn't play our own records, but the engineer wasn't even in the same building. The man who owned the station also ran a movie theater next door, and for some reason the engineer was located in the theater projection booth. We kept in touch with each other by way of an intercom system. The only problem was that the intercom was not rigged to cut off automatically when you were talking on the air. The engineer would keep saying things during performance. His remarks couldn't be heard on the air because the volume was low, but it was loud enough for *you* to hear it. While you were doing the newscast, the engineer would make all kinds of comments—some of them obscene—trying to break you up. It was funny to everybody but the audience. However, this was another workshop for learning—learning some of the things not to do as well as some of the fundamentals.

At noon it was time to grab a bite to eat, then go out and

service accounts. In other words, you picked up the chores of a salesman—visiting various sponsors to find out how they wanted their spot announcements to be done. Usually they would cut out their newspaper ads and hand them to you. Then when you got on the air, you'd simply ad-lib around the copy.

Manitowoc was a shipbuilding town and it was likable enough, but it was just too darn cold for me and I was already making plans to cut out with the spring thaw. I didn't know where I was going. The only way you found out about jobs in those days was by word being passed to you from friends at other stations, or from the help-wanted ads in the back section of *Broadcasting* magazine. Bosses usually got *Broadcasting* because it was the only trade publication—but they wouldn't let employees see it for fear they'd find a job somewhere else. Usually there were more "Situations Wanted" than "Help Wanted," but it was always interesting to see the openings for announcers that stated categorically that "drifters need not apply." Since the small stations didn't pay much money, they tried to entice you by selling the virtues of the area—"good hunting and fishing" was a common lure.

Because the magazine was off-limits to the help, I wouldn't have had access to it if it weren't for the cleaning lady—an old Indian woman who became my friend and would sneak the copies out of the boss's office. But during that cold winter, I saw no prospective jobs and I didn't pursue any.

I kept at the business of learning my trade. In those early days of radio at small stations, we seemed to be working all the time. We'd even spend our off-hours working on special programs because doing that was more fun than almost everything else. We would talk about nothing but radio, which must have been terribly boring to any outsiders who stumbled into our conversations. We just felt lucky to be in a business that was so upbeat and public spirited.

The work carried me quickly through that frigid winter and when spring arrived, I quit. I didn't even wait to find another job—which is always the smartest thing to do. I just went home to Buffalo to begin my search there.

There was a new station going on the air in Erie, Pennsylvania. Even before it was operating, I went there and auditioned, but the manager never let me know one way or the other whether I was hired. So I found a job at WHLD in Niagara Falls—at the top of the Hotel Niagara. I wasn't there two weeks when the manager of the new station in Erie showed up in person to sell me on the idea of going to work for him. I was pretty impressed by this mountain coming to Mohammed, and Erie sounded like it was a lot bigger time than Niagara Falls—so off I went.

Once again I was the morning man. I didn't realize then that the morning and I would become such inseparable companions in the years to come. Let me say something at this point about morning radio. It's not for everyone. It takes a certain kind of metabolism to get up at 3:45 A.M. every day of your work week. I know some very talented people whose bodies cannot take it. They are night people, or day people, but they can't be operating on all cylinders early in the morning. If management gave them the early-morning shift, they'd quit and find a job elsewhere.

Anyway, once again I was doing the morning show—working by myself. And it was here that I began using my various voices—impressions that would become an important part of my act later on. It was a way of building a cast of characters for my program and giving it the kind of variety that most solo performers just can't establish. Here were born The Woman, The Old Man, The Tough Guy and The Teenager.

There was a little balcony over the entrance to the station, and often I would take my microphone, crawl out on the canopy and do the show from there. It was a corny little gimmick, but people would drive by and blow their horns at this weirdo on the roof whose voice they could hear on their car radios. For the first time, I was becoming a personality and getting mail from listeners. And it was in Erie that I learned the value of personal contact with members of the community. I was becoming involved in local activities, MC'ing various events, speaking at service clubs, visiting high schools—making all the personal appearances that go with the territory of the radio personality. Life was on the upswing. My career was really launched—nothing could stop me now!

Then the bottom dropped out. Very often I used to drive back to Buffalo to visit my family on weekends. It was a ninety-mile trip—not too long. But on this particular day in 1941, I had put in a lot of hours at the station and I guess I was a little more tired than usual.

I was tooling along on the Lake Road, beside Lake Erie. It was a cold night, so the windows were rolled up and the heater was on. Just outside Lackawanna, a suburb of Buffalo—almost home—I fell asleep at the wheel. It was days before I found out what happened. The car had left the road and rammed into a stone wall. In a way that was fortunate, because a hundred feet behind that wall, the cliff dropped off three hundred feet down into the lake. There was another fortunate thing—a police car was right behind me. The officers had seen my car start to weave, and they had pulled in behind me and were sounding the horn or siren to get my attention. Obviously that didn't work, but as soon as my car struck the wall, they were able to radio for help immediately. An ambulance took me to Our Lady of Victory Hospital in Lackawanna in very critical condition: a concussion, severe lacerations and a compound fracture of my left leg. I was unconscious for three days. During that time, doctors had decided that my leg had to be amputated. My father was asked to sign the papers authorizing the surgery—but he refused. He insisted that they try to save the leg. The doctors tried to explain that my life was in danger, but my father insisted on another try. In frustration I guess they went back and worked on the leg, and somehow circulation was reestablished and the leg stayed with me.

Those were the days when hospital staffs didn't try to get you up and moving too quickly. I was there seven weeks. Then I was home in bed for another seven weeks. During that time, I became a minor celebrity. There were accounts of the accident in all the newspapers. I received hundreds of cards and letters from listeners. People would stop by to see me and bring cakes and other goodies. I had a lot of time to think in the hospital. If my maturity came in stages, that was certainly one of the times when it lurched ahead. Religion hadn't figured much in my life—I wasn't a churchgoer and I had never thought much about it. In that hospital bed it occurred to me that if the accident hadn't killed me, neither was it an accident that I was still alive. However, the incident didn't trigger any instant faith either. Religion did get to play an important part of my life—but that was some time later.

About five months went by before I was ready to report back to work. And I wasn't very mobile at that because steel plates were built into my shoe. When I stood up the steel would lock in place, which would allow me to walk stiff-legged. Then to sit down I had to flip a release that allowed my knee to bend. To make things easier, I took a room at the YMCA, which was only a half block from the radio station.

As soon as I returned to the station, it became apparent that things weren't the same. While I had been gone, management decided to make some changes and there was every indication that the changes would be drastic. It wasn't long before co-workers were getting their notices and new people were arriving. It looked like it would be epidemic. I had a week's vacation and was back in Buffalo when the manager telephoned me and told me it was not necessary to come back. They had terminated me and would send me my final paycheck. Radio station management always likes to sever relationships surgically by paying you off instead of letting you work out the usual two-week notice. They always find it a little awkward to have you around once you no longer fit into their picture. Then there is always the possibility, too, that you will poison the mind of the person they hired to replace you. So this firing was not unusual—except that it's not normally done by telephone. You usually get a chance to clean out your desk—if you were fortunate enough to have a desk.

This whole business was a severe blow to my pride. I was twenty-one years old and I had never been fired before. Later, with experience, I would learn to accept the inevitable when it came. But I was having none of that then. I wanted explanations. How could they fire *me?* I was so conscientious. I was sober. I really worked hard at my job. I was serious about my career. I was no drifter. I tried to get an explanation over the telephone, but the best the manager could offer was "You just don't fit into the picture here."

But of course I knew I *did* fit into the picture. I was popular. I had received all those cards and letters in the hospital. What did they mean, I didn't fit into the picture? I wasn't going to take this sitting down.

Station WERC was owned by three attorneys. I called them and said I wanted to talk. They agreed to see me. They knew they could handle me with dispatch. So I trundled over and told them that I was really hurt—that I wanted to know why I was being let go and all that. The attorneys were very solicitous and patiently explained the facts of life to me. They told me that a manager must be allowed to manage—to choose his own personnel without interference from the owners. They were sure that I had a bright future in the business, but it obviously wasn't with their radio station. They wished me all the luck in the world—as they walked me to the door.

Today I think, "What a young guy doesn't know." At that time I thought, "Where do I go now?"

A friend of mine, Johnny Bradford, who had worked with me at the Erie station, was now at WFMJ in Youngstown, Ohio. I decided to take a run over there and touch bases with him to see if he knew of any openings. For some reason, when I arrived in town I went first to another station—WKBN—and applied for a job. There they put me through an audition immediately and afterward offered me a job starting in two weeks. I said, "All right" and went over to WFMJ to see Johnny Bradford and tell him the news. When I walked into the station, it knocked me out. It was beautiful. It was a dream radio station—first-class equipment, elegant appointments—I *had* to work there. Johnny said, "I don't know if there's an opening, but they're always looking for talent." He arranged an audition after which the manager said, "Fine. When can you start?"

I had arrived in town without a job. Now I had two. Both had offered the same pay—around $45 a week. But WFMJ was so classy there was only one way I could go. I called the manager of the other station, told him the story and that I had decided to quit the job before I even worked there. He said something like "That's show business," and that was that.

Just as I had to learn that managers need not supply reasons for changing personnel, so, too, did I learn that performers need to be opportunists. When your career is at stake, you'd better make decisions based on what's best for you—without worrying about the effect those decisions might have on the company. I don't know of any radio station that went out of business because some employee left.

Once again I was the morning man. I spent nearly two years at WFMJ. I was still perfecting my character voices. It was there that I did my first "Big Band remote" from a theater in Youngstown, featuring Tommy Dorsey's band and a young vocalist by the name of Frank Sinatra. I didn't foresee then that "band remotes"—dance-band music broadcast from locations other than the station—would occupy so much of my time as an announcer during the war years.

I was in Youngstown when I got a call to report to the Cleveland induction center for an Army physical. I had to take the day off and go by train to Cleveland. My leg was still in a cast from the auto accident, so the Army flunked me. I was classified 4-F and they never called me back again. The Cleveland induction center was the closest I ever got to the war as far as military service was concerned.

I was doing a little bit of everything at the station, including singing, which was strange since I really can't sing very well. But some guy, who had a small combo, approached me with an idea for a radio program. He would play the piano and I would sing. We worked up a show, and the station actually gave us two fifteen-minute spots on the air. I didn't feel so great about it, but somehow the shows survived for a while.

It was also while doing the morning show at WFMJ that I first heard of WMAL in Washington. Station WFMJ was an affiliate of the Blue Network of the National Broadcasting Company, and each morning at eight, from the studios of WMAL in Washington, D.C., we would get Martin Agronsky and the news. I did the local cut-ins on the Agronsky show, but I always daydreamed that I was the network announcer on that show, working in Washington. Washington was very much in my thoughts.

As a veteran broadcaster, I was reading *Broadcasting* magazine rather blatantly now, and one day I saw an ad for WMAL. They were looking for an announcer or something, and when I saw it, my heart beat a little faster. I told a co-worker, Ken Evans, "I think I'll take a crack at this."

I put an audition on a wire recording—there was no tape yet—and sent it off to WMAL. It wasn't long before I got a call from Washington. I'm not even sure who called, but he said, "If you can report for work in one week, the job is yours." They didn't even want to interview me. They were hiring me on the basis of that wire recording. Strange things happened in those days.

I went to the manager and told him I was leaving and could only give one week's notice. He gave me a sermon about how that was a violation of the traditional two weeks' notice, but that he would try to get along without me despite my ingratitude. Thinking back on how I was fired by telephone in Erie, I wasn't very sympathetic.

Washington! Finally I was going to one of the top ten markets in radio. This was big stuff. No more transmitters with blinking lights in the middle of the floor. WMAL was a station that fed programs to the entire Blue Network of NBC. If I was going to make it someday as a network announcer, this would be a place to start. Then it would be, move over, Ben Grauer and Milton Cross and Jack Costello and Andre Baruch—I'm one of you guys!

It was a wartime Washington I reported to on March 1, 1943. And I was impressed with all that activity. Outside Union Station a taxi dispatcher put you in a cab with other people going in your direction. This was the tip-off to life in a city that was bursting at the seams.

Station WMAL was housed in the Trans-Lux Building at Fourteenth Street and New York Avenue, along with WRC.

In the early days NBC owned what were known as the Red and Blue Networks. The Red Network was the regular entertainment network, the one that made the money. The Blue provided mainly talk and was mostly noncommercial. Often NBC owned two stations in a market—one Red and one Blue. Then in 1940, after an antitrust battle, Edward Noble bought the Blue Network and turned it into the Blue Network of the American Broadcasting Company. Even after the split, NBC provided the engineering for both networks, and everything still came from the Trans-Lux Building, which was a kind of miniature Radio City.

The first thing I learned when I checked in was that the man I was replacing was still there working for a couple of days. That gave me a plan. I introduced myself to him and asked him where he was living. He said he had a room near Chevy Chase Circle. I asked if it would be possible for me to take over his room when he left. (I figured if I had his job I might as well take his room too; housing was a real problem in wartime Washington.) He took me back to that house with him, the landlady didn't seem to have any objections, so the deal was made right then and there. I took a room in a hotel for a couple of days until he moved out, and then I was all set.

Washington was a pretty glamorous place to me. I took up my duties rather wide-eyed about the whole thing. I was twenty-three years old and felt I'd come a long way from Manitowoc, Wisconsin. My Homburg wouldn't look so funny here!

Frank: Meantime, Back in Macon, Georgia

I think there's some kind of skeleton in my family closet—some secret that was kept under the rug and eventually was lost.

At any rate my ancestry is rather difficult to trace because none of my father's siblings are alive and my mother had no true siblings. She was adopted—which is not so unusual—but she was adopted by the same family that had adopted her father. That's where the plot thickens because my mother and grandfather thereby became stepbrother and stepsister. Are you still with me?

Let's go back a bit—to things as they were (or were purported to be) in Henry County, Alabama, in the southeastern part of the state. As the story goes, my grandmother, Mattie Searcy, was married when she was around sixteen to a guy named Blaylock—no one remembers his first name. It wasn't long before she had a baby—my mother, Maude. My grandparents weren't too attached to Henry County, so one day they got the bright idea to board a riverboat on the Chattahoochee River and head for Florida to seek their fortune. When they got to Florida, my grandfather got into a gunfight and was shot dead. The survivors, no longer having any reason to be in Florida, went back to Alabama. Mattie—still a teenager and with the baby—didn't have any people who could take her in. So she went to the Scott family, which had adopted her husband. Pretty soon Mattie married again and left my mother also to be adopted by the Scott family. Maude Blaylock became Maude Scott. Meantime, my grandmother married again and had some additional children. These are the relatives who are familiar to me, and they are the ones who tell me the stories. So what I have really is a lot of legends, and I think over the years it was a question of sweeping things under the rug. I don't suppose it was anything more eyebrow-raising than a lack of ecclesiastical blessing on a relationship, but it caused at least an eighteen-and-a-half-minute gap in my tape.

Things are a little simpler on my father's side. John Hall Harden was born in Georgia. All his siblings are dead, so I can't do much tracing there. But he came to Alabama for some reason or another and met Maude Scott and they got married. I was born in Macon, Georgia, on October 28, 1922.

My father had gone to work for the Central of Georgia Railroad when he was thirteen—helping the station agent in Alabama. He was working for the same company as a dispatcher in Savannah, Georgia, when he died nearly fifty years later. No drifter he.

During the Depression, he was laid off and put on something the railroad called the "extra board," which meant he worked only when they called him. He was getting only two or three days of work a month, so the family's financial situation—never princely—became rather grim. They lost the house they were making payments on, and we moved into a three-room apartment in someone else's house. Finally in 1932 my father got a full-time job as a dispatcher in Cedartown, Georgia, and we moved there. About a year later, when the economy picked up a little, we moved to Savannah. There was then, as now, no city like Savannah to me. I loved it the minute I got there, and I still have a love affair with it. It's a way of life that has for me something rare and permanent in it. Even after all these years I still go back with a great deal of anticipation.

If there was one thing of special importance that happened in the pre-Savannah days, it was the discovery that I couldn't see very well. This became obvious to those around me when I was less than two years old because I was bumping into a lot of things. It happened so often that it couldn't be dismissed as mere clumsiness. Finally they hauled me off to a doctor, and I began wearing glasses as a toddler; and I've been dependent on them ever since.

Because of the glasses—which looked like Coke bottles—I could tell on the first day of school every year which kids I was going to have to fight: the ones who called me names because of those glasses. My eyes were to present certain problems for me in later years, since I had to stay out of all competitive athletics.

Bad eyes notwithstanding, I learned my ABCs in a rather unique way. My mother spent a lot of time with me when I was a preschooler. But she had certain chores to do, so I had to amuse myself. While she would fix breakfast for my father, who would be coming home from a shift at the railroad, I'd play around on the kitchen floor. There was a cast-iron stove that had a lot of writing carved on the bottom of it, and I would study those letters and ask questions about them. What the inscription said was:

HUMPHREY STOVE COMPANY
TOLEDO, OHIO
PATENT APPLIED FOR

It wasn't the whole alphabet—but it gave me a running start. Then my mother used the headlines of the morning newspaper to build my repertoire of letters, and by the time I got to school I could already read simple words. I wonder if the

Humphrey Stove Company ever knew what kind of contribution it made to Georgia literacy. I rather suspect it was a pretty good stove, too.

My father always worked at night and slept in the daytime. I guess the one thing I remember most vividly throughout my early life was my mother's saying, "Shhh—you'll wake your daddy!" I had to whisper my way through childhood when I was indoors. I was so used to it, I would whisper even when I was in someone else's house. I thought all daddies slept in the daytime.

All during my growing up—no matter where I lived—Macon, Cedartown or Savannah, my summers were spent with my mother's relatives on their farm in Alabama. The day school was out, my brother and I, or perhaps my sister and I, would board a train with a railroad pass and head for the farm. On arrival I would kick off my shoes and I wouldn't put them back on again until the summer was over and it was time to go back home. It wasn't all play—I did my share of plowing and other chores—but it provided a change of pace and I always enjoyed it.

In the Rooseveltian thirties, we were very middle class, or lower middle class by the standards then. We rented houses. I went to public schools and got average, or a little better than average, grades. I resented not being able to take part in athletics, although I won a letter one year by becoming manager of the boxing team at Savannah High School.

It was this inability to participate in athletics that got me interested in music and into the high school band. I attended a summer program of group instruction, and the school even furnished the instrument. Somehow I ended up with a trombone. The school band at Savannah was a good one and won many state honors. The band began to take up a lot of my time—maybe even too much—I used to cut classes occasionally to hang around in the band room.

By the time I was fifteen, I was proficient enough on the trombone to play in some local dance bands. I was no Tommy Dorsey. I was never the band's first choice for a gig, but I'd get a call every now and then—perhaps when the better players weren't available. I had a musicians' union card, and even the union had a marching and concert band that would get bookings on occasion. We rehearsed in a garage every Tuesday night. Playing with that band got me into trouble at school.

The St. Patrick's Day parade was a big event in Savannah, and on this occasion union musicians were paid to march in the parade. Naturally I opted to march with the union band instead of the high school band. The bandmaster took issue with that decision and complained to the principal. The principal called me in and told me if I marched with the union band, I would be dismissed from the high school organization. I argued my case, explaining that I was simply absenting myself from the high school band that day. I told him that what I was doing was making money—that if another band member stayed away to work at the A & P, there would be no question. It just happened that *my* way of making money was by marching in the union band. But he didn't buy my argument. I marched with the union and was forthwith dismissed from the high school band. After about three or four months—with the bandmaster pleading my case—I was reinstated, but it all caused a real big to-do at Savannah High School at the time.

During my grade school and high school years, I was always fascinated with radio and listened with something akin to addiction. There was a magazine called *Radio Mirror* and I couldn't wait for it to come out because it had complete program listings and stories about all the radio personalities. There was only one station in Savannah—a CBS station—and I knew all the programs, even the obscure ones like

Sigmund Spaeth—Tune Detective or *Flow Gently Sweet Rhythm.* If it was on the radio, I listened to it. It was quite an event in my life when I got my own radio in my room and I no longer had to depend on the big Majestic in the living room—the control of which I had to share with other family members. I remember with fondness even the melodramas like *Myrt and Marge,* which was the first of the major soap operas, with its theme song "Poor Butterfly." And there was *Scattergood Baines*—the old town philosopher in the little town of Coldriver. And of course we all listened to *One Man's Family,* which was fashioned after John Galsworthy's *Forsyte Saga* and became an American radio dynasty. I remember the leading character, Henry Barber, was always saying, "Mm, mm" which was not very exciting but became a kind of program trademark.

During this period I never thought of radio as a possible future career. Like music, it was another substitute for athletic activity that my bad eyesight precluded.

As a matter of fact, during my high school years I had no idea what I wanted to do with my life. The country had mobilized in 1940 when I was eighteen. Everyone my age knew it was futile to make plans too far ahead. It was a very unsettled time and, in a way, it relieved us of making any big decisions. Fate was going to take over. Soldiers were becoming a common sight everywhere. People were getting drafted . . . units were being called up . . . friends were leaving—some I would never see again.

I was thinking about going to college, mostly because that's what kids in my economic class did. The state university only cost $90 a year. But the fact is I never thought seriously about doing anything. I never had those normal boyhood desires to be a steamboat captain, fireman or railroad conductor. I was interested in music, but I realized I was going to go just so far as a professional musician and that I would never make it to the big time. Music as a career was out. It dawned on me on occasion that at some point I was going to have to do something to sustain myself. But I'd always put those thoughts aside for some other time.

In the meantime I just kept enrolling in colleges. First I went to Newberry College in South Carolina. Then it wasn't long before I was at the University of South Carolina. All this time I was also playing in dance bands. I would play one-nighters with some of the well-known bands, like Dean Hudson's and Tony Pastor's. I played at some fairly decent clubs, like the John Marshall Hotel and the Westwood Supper Club in Richmond, and at the Tavern in the Hotel de Soto in Savannah.

Playing in dance bands gave me my first contact with radio as a performer. In those days the musicians' union had what they called "minimum complement" contracts with radio stations. So I played in studio bands on occasion. As a matter of fact, I participated in what had to be one of the funniest radio programs ever. Trouble is, it wasn't supposed to be funny! I was in a pickup band that was sent to a hotel in the Adirondacks. Somehow the hotel had managed to get some air time on the local station. The afternoon we arrived, we were told we had to do a program right away. We hadn't even met three of the musicians yet, but not long after we said, "Hello," we were on the air. And we were just awful. They would have done better by having somebody from the high school recite "The Face on the Barroom Floor."

Anyhow after leaving the University of South Carolina, I didn't go anywhere for a while. But my younger brother, who had gone to Georgia Military College, told me the school was looking for someone to lead the band and give instruction, and he thought that would be a fine way for me to occupy my time. So it was off to Milledgeville, Georgia. The institution was a junior college and my tuition was free. They gave me my uniform and I was in the cadet corps. Besides leading the band, I was taking courses, and to make some money I also had my own dance band on the side, which played at the country club and at college dances.

By this time the Selective Service people were drawing a bead on me. I could feel their breath on my neck. A professional Army man at the college said to me one day, "You know you can enlist for a certain program and they have to honor that or you're out again." I asked him, "What do you have in mind?" He said he was putting together a special parachute star battalion. That sounded pretty exciting to me, so I enlisted in the reserve corps. I had to go to a civilian doctor in Milledgeville for a physical, and I was a little apprehensive about my eyesight. But he didn't do much more than feel my pulse and send me over to Camp Wheeler, and I was in the Army. It wasn't long before I was in Fort McPherson, Georgia, getting uniforms and a series of shots and all that stuff. I was in the infantry. Over hill and over dale and whatever. Then it was on to something called "pre-jump school" in Tacoa, Georgia, which was nothing more than infantry basic in double time—six weeks instead of the usual thirteen.

I got through that without too many mishaps, and then it came time for the big stuff—you know, parachutes and jumping from airplanes and flashy shoulder patches and glamour. My class was sent to Columbus, Georgia, for that phase. Only the training cycle preceding ours wasn't quite complete yet, so we had to wait. Well, in the Army they always find something for you to do—they're not going to let you just sit around—so we were sent to various clinics at the hospital to get checked out.

When I got to the eye clinic, the doctor took one look and asked, "What in the hell are you doing here?" I answered, "I'm going to become a parachutist—you know, airplanes and glamour and all that." He said, "Wrong! You're out!" I argued about my eyes. I said, "What's the problem? When you jump out of an airplane, there ain't but one way you're going to go." But he didn't buy it, and they shipped my tail to Fort McClellan, Alabama. That meant I was back in infantry basic, which was one place I didn't want to be at all. I applied for everything there was—cooks' school and bakers' school, anything—but they kept me right there. Then just as I finished the cycle, I was called in and the officer asked me, "How would you like to go to school and study Russian?" I answered, "You took the words right out of my mouth." I figured if nothing else someday I could take a crack at reading *Crime and Punishment* in the original language. I hadn't the slightest idea why I was supposed to learn Russian. But I was assigned forthwith to what was called the Army Specialized Training Corps Program. (I had applied for the program—I had applied for everything there was because I wanted out of the infantry.) So I was sent to Auburn University—Alabama Polytechnic was what it was called then—for assignment, and then it was off to the University of Pittsburgh to study Russian. But nothing is ever as it seems in the Army. I don't think I had met the instructor more than once or twice—I never even got the book issued for the course—when they abandoned the program. I hadn't even learned *nyet* yet.

Since I was there, they simply threw me into a unit that was studying engineering. I didn't know what that was all about either, but I didn't care. I was having a good time in Pittsburgh—ensconced on the fortieth floor of what was called "The Cathedral of Learning." The food was good. Then one day they announced that program was being junked, too, and that soon we would be going overseas. It was 1943.

One morning I woke up and couldn't see at all out of my

right eye. My eyesight was pretty rotten to start with, but now my right eye was a cipher. I reported to sick call, but the sergeant wasn't impressed at all. "Oh sure," he said, "now when everybody's going overseas, you're stricken with instant blindness." It was just a matter of chance that the medical officer on duty that day happened to be an ophthalmologist. He took one look at my eye and said, "Send this man to the hospital!"

I was kept at the Presbyterian Eye, Ear, Nose and Throat Hospital in Pittsburgh for about three or four weeks. I'd had a hemorrhage in my right eye that completely dislocated the retina. The techniques to deal with that kind of problem didn't exist in those days—so not much of anything was done for me. Then I was sent to an Army hospital in Butler, Pennsylvania, but they couldn't do anything there either. All I did was lie around waiting for something to happen. The eye had gone bad in December, and finally in May 1944, they gave up on ever salvaging me as a soldier fit for duty.

As a matter of fact, I predicted D-Day in Europe by the activity in that hospital. I'd been there for several months doing nothing. Then suddenly one day an orderly came in and told me to report to the colonel. The medical board of the hospital was meeting—patients would go in, then come out smiling because they'd been discharged. So finally my turn came, and I went in. There were four or five doctors assembled, majors and colonels. They got right down to cases—told me they'd reviewed my medical history, and for the convenience of the service they were going to discharge me from the Army. They asked me if I had any questions and I couldn't think of one. No argument from me this time. Way back when I had wanted to jump out of airplanes and was told I couldn't, I argued. But not this time. I was ready to pull the ripcord and jump right out of the service. And with all these guys suddenly being discharged, it occurred to me what was happening. This was May 30, 1944, and I told another patient, "You know what they're doing—they're clearing out these hospitals because D-Day is imminent and they'll need the room." D-Day came seven days later. But I was long gone.

Reading my discharge papers I noticed that I was separated from a unit at Fort Eustis, Virginia. I'd never been to Fort Eustis, Virginia. I'm not sure I'd ever heard of it—but it was all paperwork. I guess you had to be from some unit in order to be discharged, not just a hospital patient who is in a kind of limbo—so they noted Fort Eustis on the discharge paper. There was one space on the paper that read "Noncommissioned Officer." I assume they were supposed to write "yes" or "no." But they had written "never." At least they didn't follow it with an exclamation point. Another space was headed "Military Qualifications," in which was written "none." I guess that pretty well summed up my twenty-six months in the Army. Not once had I ever been recommended for Pfc. I don't think that thought had so much as occurred to any officer who ever came in contact with me.

The war still had a year to go, but I was discharged with a disability, and I returned to Savannah. The first day home, when I put on civilian clothes people started calling me 4-F or slacker or whatever. So I solved that problem by putting my uniform back on.

The Army had given me mustering-out pay of $300, but I knew that wouldn't last very long. Now I finally had to think about what I might want to do with my life.

While in the hospital I had applied to the University of Florida. I sent along my transcripts from Newberry College, the University of South Carolina, Georgia Military Academy, etc., and I wrote, "I'd like very much to get into the University of Florida." And the man wrote back, "Dear Mr. Harden: Apparently you have pursued a hodge-podge of courses leading to no definite goal." My application was rejected.

During my six-month incarceration in the hospital in Butler, Pennsylvania, a lot of community attention had been focused there. The hospital was filled with returned heroes from the North African and Italian campaigns. I shared a room with Sergeant Forrest Vosler of Rochester, New York, who had been awarded the Congressional Medal of Honor. There were lots of newspaper features in the Pittsburgh papers, visits by show-business celebrities, and the local groups did their bits for the boys in the service.

Among the groups that showed up one Sunday night in May 1944 was a girls' chorus from New Castle, Pennsylvania—about thirty miles away. And among the performers was a young lady who became the first Mrs. Harden. We met on May 14 and were married on the following July 11—some seven weeks later. It was a whirlwind romance, to say the least. No wonder it couldn't last—only twenty-five years went by before we got tired of each other.

All the time I was in the hospitals in Pittsburgh and in Butler I had done a lot of listening to the radio. There wasn't much else to do. I monitored those stations pretty carefully, and by the time I got out of the Army I figured I knew as much about radio programs as anyone else. So I thought I would just try my luck at getting a job at some station. The war was still on and there was a shortage of men, and radio stations hadn't even a notion in those days of hiring women for on-the-air work except for the so-called "women's shows"—so I hit the job market with a certain amount of confidence.

I was twenty-two years old and still in my Army uniform when I walked into WSAV in Savannah and told the owner-manager, Harben Daniel, that I wanted to be one of his announcers. He asked me the logical question: "Have you ever announced anywhere?" I told him I hadn't but that it didn't look like something I couldn't do. I have an idea that in those days anyone who could speak English and was warm to the touch was a likely candidate for an announcing job. At any rate he agreed to give me an audition. Harben gave me some news copy and some commercials, and I guess I got through them all right, because even before I was finished he came running into the studio. "You sure you never announced before?" he asked. I assured him that was the case—but that I had listened to announcers a lot and I had practiced on my own—a statement that was at least half true. Harben asked, "When do you want to start?" I said, "How about tomorrow morning?" and the deal was made. I became one of four announcers on the station and my pay was $25 a week. It wasn't a place where I was ever going to make any great amount of money. As the story goes, Harben Daniel still has $1.65 out of the first dollar he ever made. But it was a start.

I reported for work the next day, and the very first commercial spot I read on the air could have been my last. It was an unqualified, outrageous disaster. The routine in those days on small stations was for the salesman to go out and sell the spot, then write the copy—or maybe even a copywriter would do it. They didn't seem to concentrate on getting a message across as much as they tried to turn a phrase and be cute.

On the first day I was being broken in, an experienced announcer was looking over my shoulder and doing most of the work, and he said, "O.K., you read this spot in a little while." So I took the copy into the other studio and read it over and it didn't seem too much of a challenge. Finally the time came, the other announcer pointed to me and I was on the air for Stewarts' Juvenile Shoes. I was doing pretty well, feeling pretty good about it, until I got to the tag line that read, "Send a kid back to school in shoes that fit from Stewarts' Juvenile Shoe Store." (Mini-exercise: try saying that aloud two or three times.) I got into the middle of that line, spoonerisms abounded, I must have said Jew instead of shoe at least a dozen times, I think I said shit at least once, and I didn't have sense enough then to just leave it alone—I backed up and started all over again and it only got worse. When I finally finished, I said to myself, "That's it—you'd better try something else—maybe go down to the railroad and look for a job." I was sure I could say, "All aboard" without screwing it up too much.

But maybe no one was listening because even though my performance on that spot should have prompted the sponsor to cancel, I never heard anything about it.

I guess I was pretty bad as an announcer. We all had to read the news, and there was an AP radio wire that provided a pronunciation guide to help us with names and places. I would keep it right next to me. When I'd come to one of those names, I'd glance over at the pronunciation guide—but then I'd lose my place in the copy and blow about six other words. We were a combo operation, which meant we ran our own control board. That can be a little distracting—reaching out for switches and whatever while you're trying to read something intelligently on the air—but after a while you get the hang of it and it's no problem. This was an NBC station and I had to do station breaks between the network programs. In the evening we had a block of local programming—a newscast, a business report and a sportscast, and for some reason I ended up with the sportscast—sponsored by the Men's Quality Shop. In later years I was to do a parody of sportscasters under the name of Big Moose—but in those days everything I did was a pretty serious undertaking.

Every once in a while, I would go into the office of Harben Daniel and explain to him that I couldn't live on $25 a week. Savannah was booming on a wartime economy, so the station had to be making a buck. He said the government had imposed wage controls—there was nothing he could do. I told him that I was a married man and I had to have more money to support a family. We finally settled on a way for me to earn more—I would sign up for overtime that I didn't work. But it wasn't long before I found myself really working the overtime.

One day while I was in Atlanta for some reason, I ran into a man who operated a radio station, WRLD, in West Point, Georgia. We got to talking and he asked me if I'd like to work for him. It was one of those "grass is greener" moves that you make for no other reason than to earn a few more bucks. I did just about everything at WRLD, which was a little 250-watter. I was an announcer and engineer, a salesman, a copywriter, a collector—the whole works, and after six months of that I'd had it again. The next stop was a good one—WGST in Atlanta. It was a CBS station and the first union station I had experienced. My first year there I made around $9,000, which was really unheard of in those days. It was all because of talent fees. Gospel quartets were very big on WGST and they were all sponsored. Since I was the announcer on most of these shows, the talent fees really mounted up.

I was in Atlanta for around two years and as far as I was concerned I was doing quite well. But every once in a while, people in this business make a career move that's based on something other than nurturing their careers. I don't know what it was that prompted me to pull up stakes in Atlanta where I had a perfectly good job, and go to Denver to work for KLZ. Maybe it was the idea of the life-style of the "Golden West" that we found appealing. Anyway I had been doing some network programs on CBS for Atlanta, and that's how I actually auditioned for KLZ. They made me an offer and my wife and I left Atlanta.

At KLZ they told me that while the salary was only $55 a week, the opportunity for making more was unlimited. I was familiar with the talent-fee situation that had bolstered my salary in Atlanta. The only problem was, this talk of opportunities in Denver was a fairy tale. I'd been had. I worked about a year in Denver—but it was never a happy arrangement and I knew I would either quit or be fired. I was fired.

The very day I left KLZ I went to see a record distributor, who gave me a job immediately selling records on a commission basis. We both knew this was a temporary thing until I could get back into radio. One Sunday I was listening to the radio and I heard an old friend of mine doing a program out of WMAL, Washington, D.C. I hadn't seen or talked to Charlie Edwards in quite some time—but I thought maybe I ought to give him a call and ask him if he knew of any openings in Washington. That thought no sooner flashed through my head when the telephone rang. Of course, it was Charlie. He said, "There's an opening here, baby." I told him, "Charlie, I can't get there from Denver to take an audition." He said, "Send a disk right away—that'll be good enough."

Since I no longer worked at a radio station, cutting an audition disk presented a problem. I was not very welcome at KLZ, so that was out. However, I knew some people over at KMYR, another Denver station, and the chief engineer said he'd try to sandwich me in between other things he was doing. It was the Christmas season and the station was very busy—choirs were coming in to record and there was all kinds of activity. So I grabbed some news copy and two or three commercials and read them cold. In the days when there was no tape, you made an acetate recording. I never even listened to the playback. I wrapped up the disk and shipped it off immediately to Hal Stepler, who was the chief announcer at WMAL. It seems incredible that your whole career can be on the line on the basis of a couple of minutes of hastily thrown together material on an acetate disk. You always have the feeling they may throw the disk aside with hundreds of others and you'll never hear from them again. But in this case it wasn't long before I got a call from Stepler. He told me the job was mine if I could start at WMAL by Christmas. I said, "I'll be there!"

The first thing I had to do was sell the house we had bought in Denver. Right after World War II that was no big problem. We got a contract on it almost immediately after putting it up for sale. We packed everything we could into my 1946 Buick and drove across country—trying to beat a snowstorm that was also heading east. My wife's folks lived in Youngstown, Ohio, at that time, so when we got that far, she and our infant son debarked there and I continued on to Washington, arriving Christmas Eve, 1947. I checked into the YMCA at Seventeenth and G streets, N.W., all set to begin my career at WMAL.

HARDEN AND WEAVER GALLERY

FRANK: Senator, there's something I'd like to ask.

SENATOR: What's that?

FRANK: The Congress got under way yesterday—

SENATOR: We were brilliant.

FRANK: Now why is it you people will wait until the very last minute, and then try to railroad everything through?

SENATOR: Well, we are procrastinators par excellence.

FRANK: I know you are.

SENATOR: We have learned that in the confusion of the last minutes we can sneak a whole lot through that normally would never make it—especially little rinky-dink bills that feather your own nest.

FRANK: You blow several billion dollars around like it's feathers.

SENATOR: That's traditional.

FRANK: Wouldn't it be better to start early and work on the important bills—setting priorities? You know, the public is catching on to this.

SENATOR: We hate to see that.

FRANK: Why don't you make a New Year's resolution. Right after the President's "State of the Union"—you get right down to business.

SENATOR: Well, I'll suggest that. But it'll never go farther than lunch.

Jackson: Life Among the Monuments

As soon as I was established at WMAL, I went after the thing that had brought me into radio in the first place—acting in radio dramas. I checked in with advertising agencies and the other stations where they had dramas and let them know that I was pretty good at dialects and could create characters. It wasn't long before the word got around that I could handle all kinds of acting parts. This was the way I could really supplement my income, and WMAL didn't mind as long as it didn't interfere with my regular announcing chores.

One program that I did regularly on another station was called—if you can believe it—*The Websters of Wartime Washington*. It was a once-a-week half-hour show attempting to portray the lighter side of life in wartime Washington. I played the part of a teenager who was sweet on the daughter of some Washington bigwig. Then there was *Janis Gray, Government Girl*. That show was a regular soap opera on WJSV, the CBS station that later became WTOP. Janis Gray was always getting mixed up in some kind of intrigue involving politicians who were always in hot pursuit of her.

Around fifteen or twenty of us did all the acting work in Washington—it became kind of an exclusive club. I suppose it was tough on people trying to break in and win acting roles; but the directors had to whip these shows out in a hurry and it was easier for them to keep using the people they knew could do the job without a lot of fuss and bother. They also used me to teach dialects to other actors. For example, one show called for someone to speak with an Italian accent, which he just didn't have. The actor was Ross Martin, who became famous later on in television playing Mr. Lucky and acting in *The Wild, Wild West*. But I had to give him his Italian accent for that particular show.

Of course, my bread-and-butter job was announcing. I still figured this was how I was going to climb into the big time. I arrived at WMAL just after NBC cut free its Blue Network, which later became reorganized as the Blue Network of the American Broadcasting Company. But we were still all together in the Trans-Lux Building. With World War II under way and no way of getting new broadcasting equipment, NBC provided engineering services not only for its own station, WRC, and its own network but also for WMAL and the ABC network. So we had our own announcer at WMAL, but we worked out of NBC studios using NBC engineers. The programming and sales staffs were completely separate—engineering and maintenance were done by our staff. And although we shared studios—for example, we would use Studio A and NBC would use Studio B—we didn't interchange them.

During the war years there were all kinds of opportunities to do special shows. One of my favorite jobs was as backup announcer on a program called *Victory Parade of Spotlight Bands*—they went in for long titles in those days. This was a network program sponsored by Coca-Cola. It featured a big band each night and originated from different military bases. An announcer would cover appearances on the West Coast, another the Midwest and a third the East. I was called in on occasion when the regular East Coast announcer couldn't make it. The very first one I did was from Newport News, Virginia, and I did quite a few of them during the next two years. It was a big deal for me—my very first coast-to-coast network show. I'd fly or take a train to the various military posts and go directly to a rehearsal where they'd have a script waiting. It was my job to introduce all the band numbers, we'd run through it all getting the show timed, and then we'd go live the next day.

Victory Parade of Spotlight Bands actually started on the Mutual Radio Network in 1941 as a fifteen-minute show. The idea was to take the country's favorite bands to the various scenes of wartime domestic activity. The Saturday night slot would go to the most popular band in the nation as determined by record sales. The Blue Network had picked up the show after Mutual dropped it, and in 1943 the Saturday night show was eliminated, and the program became a thirty-minute, five-nights-weekly show.

This was the era of course of the big bands, and network announcers spent much of their time doing remotes from the dance pavilions like the Glen Island Casino in New York, or supper clubs like Frank Daley's Meadowbrook in Cedar Grove, New Jersey.

Another thrill for me as a young broadcaster was when I was a spear carrier on *The U.S. Steel Hour*—one of the big network drama shows. This program also went on location for its live broadcasts from time to time. On one occasion it came to Washington's Constitution Hall and featured Elizabeth Taylor and Spencer Tracy in "Father of the Bride." I played a butler—not one of my more memorable roles. But I remember Elizabeth Taylor, who was quite young at the time, and her mother, who kept by her side to protect her from the Don Juans. (Not many months ago I was at a fund-raising affair for a Vietnam Veterans memorial, hosted by Senator John Warner and his wife at that time, Elizabeth Taylor. I got to chat with her and reminded her of that long-ago appearance of "Father of the Bride." She remembered the radio play well, but she had no recollection at all of the butler!)

I was also hired to do *The Bob Hope Show* during that period. The program—sponsored by Pepsodent—had the highest Hooper rating of all shows in 1943 and remained one of the powerhouses of radio. Hope took the program to various cities, and when he came to Washington they hired me to play a senator. They needed some extras, got in touch with the union, and I was sent over to the Hotel Statler to do the show. We rehearsed all day—the program then featured Jerry Colonna and Frances Langford, and I think Desi Arnaz had the band. But one thing I noticed right away was that no matter what Hope said during the rehearsal—everybody laughed. I mean, if somebody said, "It's raining out" and Hope said, "Oh yeah?" everybody would fall on the floor laughing. It wasn't hard to figure out why. When you are Bob Hope, the laughs are guaranteed no matter what you say. Maybe the writers of the show were leading the laughter. Not that he needed any of it—Hope was and remains one of the sharpest comedians of all time.

When the director was briefing me on my part, he warned me that if Hope began to ad-lib—I should not take him on. He said, "He'll cut you to pieces." But as the show went on, I felt at ease, and I was hoping that maybe he would wander from the script a bit. I've always felt pretty confident in an ad-lib situation and I thought no matter what he said, I could come up with something of my own. But I never got the opportunity. He stuck to the script. Obviously, he had been forewarned about my sharp-edged ripostes and chose not to do battle with me!

Another time I was hired to participate in *Gene Autry's Melody Ranch*—one of the longest-running shows in the history of radio broadcasting. It featured songs and banter, and a highlight was a ten- to fifteen-minute story narrated by Autry and dramatized by a cast. We did this on the stage of the Capitol Theater; the following week the show moved to Baltimore and I went along, too. The only thing I remember is that Autry had a hard time carrying a tune. The guitar player would stand there next to him and keep plunkin' out the melody until he got it. And once he got it, he kept it.

This was also the period when I finally got to sea. Well, not really. I got as far as the Navy Yard. Each week on the Blue Network there was a live broadcast from the Sail Loft at the Yard. It was called *The Navy Hour* and featured music—the top singers from the big bands.

It was also during this time that I began my association with the Forest Service in the U.S. Department of Agriculture. One day the Service called me and asked me for my impression of what a bear would sound like if it spoke like a human. They had a cartoon bear they were going to use in a big promotional campaign to help fight forest fires, but they didn't have a voice to go with it. I volunteered a few bear voices, and they invited me over to see what I could do. I went to the U.S. Recording Studios; by this time I had the voice pretty well down pat, so I gave them a sample. At first I used a wastebasket for the proper resonance. That's how I became the voice of Smokey the Bear, who would develop into one of the most famous advertising symbols in the world. I don't know how many times my voice was heard saying, "Only you can prevent forest fires." Many years later I got a call from a commercial outfit doing a series of TV cartoon shows called *The Adventures of Smokey Bear*. They had the approval of the Forest Service and asked me if I could come up to Toronto where they were taping the series and do the voice of Smokey. So each Saturday for two months or so, I flew to Canada, taped around five or six shows and flew back to Washington. I guess the program ran for a couple of years. I think the reason they did the show in

Canada was to ensure coverage in that country. Canada has a rule that a certain percentage of TV shows seen there must be Canadian made.

We had other duties as well. The ABC network news bureau and the WMAL news staff consisted of, I think, four people, aside from the commentators. Many of the things that news people do now announcers had to do then. Once I was sent to the White House. I was smoking cigars at that time and had one in my teeth when I entered the grounds. One of the in-house guards came over to me and said, "Would you mind putting that out? The First Lady doesn't like cigar smoke."

We would traditionally send an announcer to the opening of Congress or when someone special was to address the members. Of course, microphones weren't allowed on the floor, but we would go to the cloakroom and set up our equipment and broadcast what we could see by looking through the transom while standing on a ladder. I was sent over there once when Winston Churchill was addressing a joint session. Bryson Rash, who would later become a well-known newsman, was one of our radio coordinators. Since I was new in town, Rash explained to me about getting up on the ladder and looking through the transom. I did so and was extremely impressed by the goings-on, but I didn't have the foggiest notion of what was happening or who was doing what. Bryson said, "Don't worry—I'll go in and get information and pass it along to you and you'll have no trouble with the broadcast." Well, he left, and when the broadcast got under way he was nowhere to be found. I struggled for about fifteen minutes before Churchill finally was introduced and began to speak. That's when Bryson showed up with some scribbled notes that I couldn't have read even if he'd brought them to me on time. Bryson became a distinguished newscaster in later years. He had no trouble reading his *own* notes.

* * *

And when during all of this did I meet Frank Harden?

I wish I could say that it was some kind of memorable occasion when he joined the staff in late 1947. But to tell you the truth, I haven't the foggiest idea how it came about. I'm sure we were introduced—or maybe we introduced ourselves after bumping into each other in a hallway. But you would have had a hard time convincing me that my career in Washington would be so closely associated with his. However it was that we met, destiny did not whisper in my ear, nor did a montage of scenes to come flash before my eyes. He probably said something like "How ya doin'?" But I didn't record it in my diary. As a matter of fact, I never kept a diary. I never intended to be *that* famous. And by golly, I was right!

Frank: Station Brake

In the early days of radio when the networks chose announcers they didn't hold any big talent search. I have an idea they were picked from the ranks of those who wanted the job and kept making that fact known. The people who had the plum announcing jobs—the big shows—were those who had auditioned for them. The original cast of announcers from New York—David Ross, Harry Von Zell, Ben Grauer, Milton Cross, Jack Costello, Andre Baruch, set the standards for the industry. They had strict dress codes: No one showed up for work after 6:00 P.M. without a tuxedo.

In Washington, working for a station that was very closely associated with the network gave you many opportunities for getting network assignments. In fact, there were many days when we had nothing but ABC assignments. So I was feeling pretty good about what I was doing. I was the announcer on network news programs such as those done by Elmer Davis, Baukhage and Martin Agronsky. I was rather in awe of this assignment except on payday. My newfound eminence was reflected everywhere except in the accounting department. Outside of what talent fees I could muster, my pay as specified in the American Federation of Radio Artists (AFRA) scale was $55 weekly.

It certainly wasn't backbreaking work. We had ten announcers, and many times my whole day would include nothing more than a few station breaks, a network program and maybe a remote. You spent a lot of time sitting on your fanny waiting for that inevitable pause for station identification. Each day when you came to work you had to check the assignment sheet made up by the chief announcer.

We had several guys at one time or another who drank quite a bit—but their buddies would always cover for them. One announcer was there for about eight months and management didn't know he drank—until one day he came in sober. Guys would go off on a toot for as long as three days, but management didn't know the difference just so the announcing schedule was covered. There was no problem as long as the chief announcer went along with the routine. Every once in a while something would mess up and an edict would be issued declaring that there would be no more covering for people who weren't there. This happened once at WRC just when announcer Holly Wright had made plans to go to Philadelphia to see the Army-Navy football game. Holly wrestled with his soul for a long time and decided finally, in spite of the memo, to take off for Philadelphia and let somebody cover for him. This was in the early 1950s and it happened to be the first time the zoom camera was used in television coverage of the game. There were 104,000 people at the game, but wouldn't you know it? they zoomed in on a spectator, and there was Holly Wright having a great time when he was supposed to be back in Washington making station breaks.

I was the announcer on the Edward P. Morgan news program on ABC—sponsored by the AFL-CIO. The program always opened with me saying, "Fifteen million Americans bring you Edward P. Morgan and the news." Well, there came a time when the AFL-CIO threw out the Teamsters Union. That cut the membership down to thirteen and a half million, and we had to change the copy accordingly.

One night Morgan was doing the program from somewhere else—but I was announcing as usual from the studios in Washington. His secretary was acting as producer—keeping track of the time and everything—and she was very uptight about it. She kept changing her mind about what the word cue for switching was supposed to be. With about thirty seconds to go, she must have handed me fourteen different notes and whispered to me about ten times. When she finally cued me, I said, "Thirteen and a half Americans bring you Edward P. Morgan and the news!" Coast to coast.

Another time I was assigned as the announcer on the Elmer Davis news program on ABC. Mr. Davis was a real scholar and a gentleman in every sense of the word. We did the program at 7:15 every evening in Studio D of the old Trans-Lux Building. The engineer and I had come to expect Mr. Davis's arrival in the studio at about ten after seven because that's what had happened every evening in memory. Well, one night about five minutes before Mr. Davis's usual arrival, the engineer and I were having a refreshing pull from a handily secreted container of Imperial Blend (in those days no studio was without its handy little hiding place) when in walked Elmer Davis. Being fast on my feet, I asked him, "Mr. Davis, do you care for a small libation?" "No, thank you," Mr. Davis responded. "And I think you'll find the literal meaning of libation is 'to pour upon the ground in ceremonial fashion' and that, I think, would be a dreadful waste of good booze."

Whenever a sponsored program came along, there would be a competitive audition to see who would win the program and the extra fee that it provided. It could be a network show or perhaps a syndicated program like *Boston Blackie* or *The Wayne King Show*.

At the end of the day we would all gather at Burt's Trans-Lux Restaurant downstairs—the main watering hole and meeting place of the fraternity. Assembled were people from

NBC, ABC, WRC and WMAL—all the stations that operated out of that building. There would be conversation involving the likes of Morgan Beatty, Elmer Davis, Earl Godwin and Baukhage. And every once in a while, we would share the room with a young photographer from the *Washington Times-Herald* by the name of Jacqueline Bouvier. But she kept pretty much to herself.

Because of the way NBC and ABC operated—with engineers in common and shared facilities—the announcers became good friends. I remember during Harry Truman's inauguration, an NBC announcer and I were sent out to the National Guard Armory. We drove there together in his car, and since there was no parking place, I told him I would go in and tell his producer and engineer that he would be along soon. So I went in and touched bases with my own people and then checked with the NBC producer. It soon became evident that there was no way my colleague was going to find a parking space and get there in time. So I did the opening for our show on ABC—while NBC was carrying the music from the bandstand—then I went over and did the opening for NBC. This didn't happen very often—only in emergencies—but it's something that could never be done today.

Announcers had strange quirks. I worked with one guy who seemed normal enough, but he was scared to death to go on the network. When his name would appear on the schedule to do a network spot, he would hide in the men's room. Everybody would cover for him, so there was no problem, and after a while the chief announcer simply didn't assign him to any network shows.

One day we got a call from the police asking us if we had an announcer named Harry something. He was new on the job and no one was really sure, but we went down anyway and bailed him out of jail. He'd been arrested at Griffith Stadium for screaming obscenities at the ballplayers.

There was another Harry—I don't remember his last name

either—who got into an argument with his wife one day and knocked her down a flight of steps. She died of her injuries and Harry was thrown in jail. A lot of his colleagues went to court to testify as to his character, and he was finally acquitted. We all went to the Roma Restaurant for Harry's "coming-out" party.

We used to have an arrangement with the Trans-Lux Theater in which we did a short newscast for theater patrons during a break between features. We were paid fifty cents for each of these newscasts, and we pooled all the money and divided it later. One day a new announcer joined the staff. We explained the routine, including the newscast downstairs at the Trans-Lux Theater, and showed him the piggy bank where we put the fifty cents. As far as I know, this announcer never worked on the air, and when he took off he absconded with the money in the kitty. If there was $3.50 in that piggy bank, I'd have been surprised.

Another announcer who worked briefly for WMAL was the son of a musical-comedy star. He had only been with us for about three days when he got on the TWX (the teletype machine) and tapped out some thoughts about the station to his buddies in New York. He apparently didn't care much for WMAL or its management, and he put it all in that message. It was really a blistering indictment based on his three days of experience. Well, for some reason or another—quite possibly due to an absence of brains—he left his little essay on the machine when he finished. The girl whose job it was to distribute the TWX material to the appropriate managers proceeded to do just that when she came in the next morning. She didn't even read it ahead of time. That was the end of him.

When the President was going to speak, every network would send an announcer to the White House—that meant four announcers. There was a regular format for the broadcast which gave us something like twenty-two seconds to introduce the President. We had to end the introduction with "Ladies and gentlemen, the President of the United States." Well, the four announcers all knew each other. We'd get together and agree that we would keep our voices down so we wouldn't get on the other guy's broadcast. Everybody was crowded into a small area, and it was difficult to keep from being heard by someone else. Despite all the agreements, every time the President stepped to the podium, the announcers would start out sotto voce; it wasn't long before the voices would all start to rise and anybody tuned in to any of the networks could hear a quartet of voices all saying, "Ladies and gentlemen—the President of the United States."

Being sent to the White House was a big deal. When the atom bomb had been dropped on Japan and the war was winding down, an announcer and an engineer were sent over every day to stake the place out. There was no White House press office as there is today. You would just sit there on a ledge by the gate. Four or five people would be allowed inside, and they'd come out with the information and go on the air, or give the information to someone else to broadcast.

Once we had an engineer by the name of Lionel St. Peter. I was assigned to the White House one day and my engineer suddenly discovered he was missing some equipment that he needed. The station dispatched Lionel St. Peter in a cab to bring us the gear. I was supposed to run out and meet him at the gate, but I didn't get there in time. The taxi arrived and the guard telephoned with the momentous message that "Saint Peter is at the gate!"

There wasn't much coverage of spot news in those days. I remember when the attempt was made on President Truman's life at Blair House. I was just coming on shift. As was my custom, I stopped by the saloon across the street to get a shooter. When I walked in, the waitress was yelling, "Hey, did you hear what happened? They tried to shoot the President!" I went running across the street and found the news editor alone in the news room. At about that time, we heard the AP wire go "ding-ding-ding" on the teletype with the announcement of the assassination attempt. So the editor sent a newsman down there and an announcer. We didn't have any tape recorders or beeper phones or any way of getting anything live back to the studio. All we were able to do was find out whatever we could—and phone back the information that somebody else could put on the air. Or we could run back ourselves and describe what we'd seen.

The ABC-NBC marriage could get rather confusing at times. On big remotes, NBC would send out two engineers—one for ABC, the other for NBC. In fact, in master control there were loudspeakers labeled "NBC," "ABC," "WRC" and "WMAL." One master control ran the whole thing. WMAL-ABC was the first to move away from the Trans-Lux Building and went to 4461 Connecticut Avenue, N.W. By this time television was part of the operation. The radio section hadn't been completed, so we did radio programs out of the television control room. WRC-NBC moved to the old Wardman Park Hotel, where it operated out of hotel rooms and storage rooms. It was the beginning of the end of old radio in the face of television's onslaught.

On WMAL, as on most network stations, the bulk of the programming originated with the network. Local programs went on from 6:00 to 9:00 A.M., and there would be a block of women's programs at around noon along with a newscast and maybe a half hour of transcribed music, the famous "musical interlude." Then it would be back to the network again for soap operas until the early evening when the station went local again.

As we moved into the 1950s, television began to loom very

large. Programs that were on radio began swinging over to television. Network radio appeared to be going the way of the dinosaur. It was time for radio to regroup.

HARDEN AND WEAVER GALLERY

FRANK: Dr. Headcold, it's a pleasure to have you here.
DOCTOR: Thank you.
FRANK: All the way from Albino State College—directly across Route Sixty-six from Goldberg's Hacienda, overlooking the River Shannon. Happy Hour Thursday and Friday evenings from five to seven—drinks half price.
DOCTOR: You seem to know more about it than I do—and I hang out there. The faculty members go over there and get a few snifters. Makes you hum.
FRANK: How are the students in the music department coming along?
DOCTOR: Real well. We have the Advanced Symphony with us now.
FRANK: You're getting ready for—
DOCTOR: Beethoven's birthday, we're going to play—
FRANK: Hold it. Beethoven's birthday was last December.
DOCTOR: Well, yes. But that doesn't make any difference. People don't follow things that closely.
FRANK: Oh?
DOCTOR: That's a trivia thing. Why even bring it up?
FRANK: Well, what are some of the selections you'll be playing?
DOCTOR: We're going to play music from *Martha*—
FRANK: Hold it. *Martha* was written by Von Flotow.

DOCTOR: There you go again. That's trivia. People don't know that. Or care. The big problem is, we don't have a place to perform.

FRANK: What happened to the auditorium at Albino State?

DOCTOR: It's flooded—a foot and a half of water. We may make it the school swimming pool—put in competitive swimming. You see—

FRANK: Thank you, Dr. Headcold.

Jackson: TV or Not TV

Times were changing. Television was coming on strong. I figured if I couldn't beat them, I'd join them. In a way TV offered a lot of opportunities for a short, hefty fella with a big moustache and a twinkle in his eye. That's no longer true today. Nowadays if you were to take every television MC on the air and put them in the same room, their mothers would have a hard job telling them apart. They'd have to sift through the rows of perfect teeth and blow-dried hair.

Most of the programming on the local level was live. This was before the videotape revolution, and a great many of the local shows were done on the spur of the moment.

We used to do a lot of live commercials. One time there was a near disaster on the set. I was doing a beer commercial, and as part of a gimmick I had a large cornucopia of paper. It was a special kind of paper. When it was ignited it would burn so fast it turned into smoke almost immediately. What I was supposed to do was fill the paper cornucopia with beer—or at least pretend to fill it—actually I was pouring nothing into it. Then when I had it filled I had to hold it up. Out of sight of the camera I had a cigar which I was to touch to the bottom of the paper, then toss the cornucopia into the air, at which time it would go "poof" and disappear. I was to say, "That's how this beer will disappear in your house—so you'd better have plenty of it on hand when friends drop by." It had worked beautifully when we rehearsed it two or three times, but when I did it live everything fell apart. The paper didn't burn completely, and when it came down it fell on top of the counter. The counter was covered with paper that made it look like a marble top, and that paper began to burn. I was trying to talk about the beer and fight the fire at the same time. Finally I gave up the commercial and just started pounding away at the top of the table.

Live commercials provided all kinds of hazards and were also a fertile ground for practical jokers. We used to do a lot of demonstrations—especially for vacuum cleaners. I remember there was an announcer who had to do about thirty spot commercials for a $10.95 used but reconditioned model. He had the pitch down pat and he would arrive on set at the last second. One of his bits was to take a big box of baking soda and pour a whole lot of it onto a rug, then he would vacuum it to show everybody how this inexpensive machine would suck that stuff up. The temptation for the rest of us just became more than we could bear. We kept watching him perform this silly demonstration time after time, and one day we had to do it. Before he arrived on the set we reversed the hose on the vacuum cleaner. He rolled in as usual at the last second and made his pitch. Then he sprinkled the baking powder on the remnant of rug, turned on the vacuum cleaner and disappeared in a snowstorm.

Television is more refined now. Everything is on videotape to guard against error. But this perfection also produces a certain sterility. A lot of the fun is gone.

One of the early programs on WMAL-TV was *Ruth Crane, Modern Woman*. Every television station in the country had a similar show. This one had actually started on WMAL-Radio—it was a program of household hints, recipes and interviews dealing with women's problems. They put me on the program with Ruth Crane, and it was my job to provide a little humor—liven things up a bit. As she went along doing her thing, I'd make certain off-the-wall comments. Ruth was quite serious and most of what I said she found ridiculous, and she'd get a bit exasperated and say, "Oh Jackson!" like I was an incorrigible child and she was the teacher. But I guess it wasn't too bad, because when television came along in 1946, *Ruth Crane, Modern Woman* made the transition from radio and I went along with it. Like every other television station, ours had a completely equipped kitchen on the set, and we did the show from there.

From time to time, 4-H groups would appear on the show to talk about various county fairs. Once one of the groups thought it would be a great idea to have a live cow on the program. Our studios were on the upper floor of an old ice-skating rink up on Connecticut Avenue and there was no elevator. You had to climb quite a few stairs to get to the lobby. This always presented a problem when manufacturers delivered heavy broadcasting equipment—very often they'd have to use a block and tackle to get it up those two landings. I might also say that our general manager, Fred Houwink, was a stickler for cleanliness and orderliness. He would get up from his desk a couple of times a day to inspect the premises. He didn't even want people standing around who weren't supposed to be in a particular place. Whoever it was that approved the appearance of a cow in the studios obviously hadn't checked with the boss first. Well, the 4-H'ers brought the cow up the stairs, through the lobby and into the studio without any problem; Ruth and I did the show and the cow seemed in pretty good spirits. But when the animal got to the lobby and saw those stairs, it apparently decided up was O.K. but down was another story. The cow simply stopped and wouldn't budge. No amount of coaxing would encourage it to leave. There was a lot of pushing and pulling and a lot of standing around doing nothing, and by and by the cow got very nervous and left a calling card all over that highly polished mosaic-tile floor. The cow, feeling a little better now, proceeded down the stairs and the production crew managed to clean up the mess before the boss arrived on the scene.

While the Ruth Crane program was a carbon of shows everywhere, Ruth and I also launched another program that was the first of its kind in the country. Sponsored by the Hecht Company, this one was called *Shop by Television*. We would show about sixteen items—anything you'd find in a department store, mops, silverware, rugs—and live models showed dresses and sportswear. Meantime we had people stationed at telephones off the set who would take orders from the viewers. It was quite successful. We'd sell as much as five thousand dollars' worth of merchandise on a good night, which wasn't bad considering what prices were in those days.

One of the staples of local television in the early days was the kids' program that played *Our Gang* comedies or cartoons and had a live character as the host, who came on to entertain the kids at the beginning of the show and in between the cartoons and films. Actually this is still done on some independent stations. My character was called Uncle Flapjack—a name devised by the director, Frank Ford, for no other reason than it had a good sound to it. The fun of these programs was that they were more or less spontaneous. All the members of the floor crew would contribute ideas for me to do between the film bits, and we did everything. I brought my young sons to the set on occasion to perform.

Another children's show found me as Ouiji the Clown. Another announcer, George Crawford, was Oji, and we would work on alternate days—again between the cartoons and old films.

One day entrepreneur Connie B. Gay met me in the hall at the station and asked, "Jack, how would you like to do a country-music show?" I answered, "You name it, I'll do it." And Connie said, "O.K. You go down to Counts' Western Store and get yourself a western-cut suit with some toolin' around the edges, a couple of western shirts and a string tie and be ready to start next week." That was the beginning of *The Jimmy Dean Show* on Channel 7.

At the time, Jimmy Dean was in the Air Force, stationed in the Washington area, but at night he also had a band playing at various places. Connie B. Gay came up with the *Jimmy Dean Town and Country Time Show,* which became an immediate hit. I was the announcer and also a character that Dean and the others could play off, and I also did the commercials. The show was on from 6:30 to 7:00 P.M. six days a week. Monday through Friday we were in the studio, but on Saturday nights the program originated from Turner's Arena (later called Capitol Arena) at Fourteenth and W streets. The Saturday night show began at around nine or ten in the evening and stayed on the air until they felt it was time to end it. If we weren't finished by eleven, well, we'd just stay on until eleven-thirty. Things were loose then and the arena was packed every Saturday night. Gay booked in all the big acts as guest stars—many from the *Grand Ole Opry.* There was even a troupe of cloggers on the show. *The Jimmy Dean Show* was on Channel 7 for about seven years until Dean got so popular he began doing a CBS network show and then went on to New York.

Also in the late 1950s I had a ten-minute show called the *Captain Jack Weather and Fishing Report.* The program went on at around 11:00 P.M. The set had a sea motif. I would be seen standing on the deck of a boat—leaning on a railing—the boat tied to a big piling. There was a porthole behind me with a light shining from inside. I would start out by talking about the weather—in a folksy way, not like a meteorologist. A big bucket of fish would be brought to me each evening by Gus Berlitz of the Berlitz Marine Anchorage in Deal, Maryland. These were fish that had actually been caught that day, and I would hold up a blue, or whatever, and explain where it was caught. At the end of the program we could cast off; we were able to create a fairly good illusion of the boat moving away from the dock. What we really did was draw the piling back with the camera—so actually the dock was drifting away from the vessel—but it made a good effect.

Captain Jack walked the plank when WMAL-TV hired the popular weatherman Louis Allen away from WTOP.

I had done other weather shows in the past that were based more on humor than on weather. It was the same idea that paid off so handsomely for Willard Scott in later years.

Again I would seek inspiration from other people at the station for my weather shows. One time I came onto the set swinging on a rope. On another occasion I did the show from the air-conditioning ducts, which were big enough for me to enter. There was a camera sitting outside the ducts, and I would come out as a professor who had invented a weather machine that would give me a precise weather forecast. Then I would disappear back into the machine, which would shake and rattle, and I would come out with a piece of paper containing the weather forecast. A *Streetcar Named Desire* it wasn't. But we had a lot of time to fill on TV in those days and we'd try anything once.

There were an awful lot of emergencies. One time weatherman Louis Allen couldn't make his broadcast, so they rushed me onto the set to substitute for him. All I had was a little blackboard and a piece of chalk. So I started plotting the weather, not having the foggiest idea what the real weather was. I drew in a high-pressure system over there and a front over here, and I noticed that all my scribbling was beginning to look like a game of tic-tac-toe. Finally I drew a line and put three Xs and won the game. The director in the booth apparently thought all this was pretty funny, so he wasn't paying any attention to the time; then I was told I had only eight seconds left and I hadn't even given a weather forecast yet. So I said, "Oh yes, if you want to find out what the weather is going to be—dial WE 6-1212," the number of the telephone company's weather forecast. Well, the news director called me into his office and wanted to know what happened, and we had a big meeting with the account executive and the program director and everybody. There were a lot of frowns and threats about jobs being in jeopardy. But I knew in advance from the salesman that the sponsor had loved the show. So I took the blame—saying I just got carried away and didn't pay any attention to my cues, and the whole thing blew over.

I was still doing a great deal of radio, too. For a couple of years I was the announcer on the Martin Agronsky news show in the morning. This was a big kick for me because this program was the one that had made me aware of WMAL when I was at WFMJ in Youngstown, Ohio, doing the local cut-ins. Agronsky was very businesslike, and I don't think there was any real rapport between him and the announcers who did the show. The Agronsky newscast at 8:00 A.M. was the network's first program of the day, and he always arrived at the last second before the show was to go on.

One morning, as I was about to do the opening and introduce him, he wasn't there. I stretched it out a little bit, thinking that he'd be dashing in at any moment, but finally there was nothing more I could say—and still there was no Agronsky. Stations all over the country were carrying the program during the morning rush hour—and here we were offering them dead air. So I did what I thought was the only thing I could do under the circumstances. I proclaimed, "The Martin Agronsky news program, usually heard at this time, will not be on this morning." Right then I heard a great commotion in the hallway, and Agronsky came tearing into the studio all wild-eyed and sat down. I just picked it up by saying, "No—Mr. Agronsky IS in the studio now" and then I did the whole opening again to give him a chance to catch his breath and he began his newscast. Almost immediately the phone rang in the control room. It was New York, of course, and I figured I'd better take it and explain what happened. I told them the story. There were a lot of four-letter words ringing in my ears and none of them was "love."

As soon as the show was over Agronsky jumped all over me like the whole thing was my fault—as if I had been blocking the studio door or doing something to prevent him from getting in on time. Then he went to management and complained about how I had screwed up the show. His main complaint was that I had left the studio while he was on the air, which was indeed against the rules. The upshot was they took me off the show. I stayed off for a long while, but there came a time when everything was forgotten and Agronsky and I worked together again.

Then there was the Edward P. Morgan episode. Frank Harden was the regular announcer on the program which, of course, was another network show originating from the WMAL-ABC facilities in Washington. I was the standby announcer one day, so I was in one studio while Morgan and Frank operated out of another studio around the corner. I never concerned myself much when I was standby because Frank always showed up. So I did the station break that led into the program. I noticed while I was doing it that the engineer was waving at me like a crazy man, trying to get my attention. It dawned on me that he was trying to tell me that Frank had not shown up for the program and that Edward Morgan didn't have anyone with him in the other studio to put him on the air. I took off at a gallop down the hall and around the corner, and as I entered the doorway I tripped over the landing and fell flat on my face. Ed Morgan—who was always unruffled—sat there looking at me as if I had gone mad. I had about four seconds left to get up on my feet and get him on the air. Afterward he asked, with a puzzled look, "Do you always enter a studio that way?" I answered, "No—sometimes they shoot me from a cannon!"

HARDEN AND WEAVER GALLERY

FRANK: Dr. Willoughby—you are a noted marriage counselor.

WILLOUGHBY: Yes.

FRANK: You were telling me that you can spot the kinds of clients you are going to have as soon as they come through the door.

WILLOUGHBY: Yes. For example, if when they enter the wife is saying, "Shut up, knucklehead, I'll do the talking," I know I have a particular problem there.

FRANK: That's a tip-off?

WILLOUGHBY: Yes. And if someone comes in who is obviously in need of dental work—you know—missing teeth, then I know I may have to plumb the depth of my talents.

Frank: Morning Becomes Eclectic

I stayed pretty much on the radio side when television came along, keeping busy with a lot of network announcing and doing an increasing amount of morning radio. As the 1950s got under way, Jimmy Gibbons was our morning personality, but he was also very heavily into sports—he did the ABC game of the week with Harry Wismer and he did the Washington Redskins games. Therefore, he was often out of town from Friday through Monday. I would always do the Saturday program, and during the football season I would often do the Friday and Monday shows as well. Then when Gibbons went on vacation I would also be the substitute. I was the neophyte in the Washington market. Among the other morning men were Art Brown at WOL, Bill Herson on WRC and Milton Q. Ford on WWDC; and Arthur Godfrey and Eddie Gallaher were on two hours each for WTOP—though by that time Godfrey was doing his show from New York. Along with WINX, these were the only stations in town.

All the announcers on all the stations knew each other, and there was a lot of fraternizing. For one thing, there were fewer of us then than there are now, and you could free-lance on other programs as long as you didn't announce. There was more fraternity in the union, too. We only had around forty members as against the 2,400 people in the American Federation of Television and Radio Artists (AFTRA) local today. I don't even know most of the people in town now—simply because I have no occasion to see them.

Television was becoming the major force in broadcasting. The big personalities and their advertisers were shifting to TV. The network stations lost all of their live programming, and they had to redefine their mission and focus more on local issues. The network stations essentially began doing what the independent stations had been doing all along. They took up the jukebox syndrome—broadcasting recorded music. To take care of more and more of the programming, our station began importing people—trying them out for various programs. Every station could play the same music, but could be made distinctive by the personalities who became the hosts of those DJ programs. Radio was in transition. As a matter of fact, that transition continues today on a larger scale. If the fifties and sixties saw great changes, you can look forward to even more revolutionary forms in the eighties with the continuing explosion of FM radio.

WMAL-Radio was an also-ran in the fifties. The main concentration of the Evening Star Broadcasting Company was on television. The radio station wasn't a moneymaker. In fact, I don't think it was a coincidence that our paychecks were usually handed out at around two o'clock in the afternoon and couldn't be deposited in the bank until the next day. Of course, in those days the *Washington Evening Star* was the leading newspaper and had plenty of money. Its owners had no inkling that the television they were helping to nurture would change the way people would get their news so drastically that afternoon newspapers would become the chief victims. Nor did they know that their radio station—then rather dormant—would become so dominant that its revenues would be used to prop up a mortally wounded newspaper.

There were times when circumstances would put me on a

program with Jackson Weaver. Whenever that happened I think both of us got the feeling that we had a certain rapport on the air. One day the program director—Charlie Kelly—told me he had a forty-five-minute slot in the afternoon to fill and broached the idea of the two of us doing the show. We cut an audition disk, and it wasn't long before we were a team in the afternoon. We were on the air for about a year, but they kept moving our show around to accommodate other programs. The program finally was moved into the evening hours, which was really television time so no one paid much attention to it. Except us. We thought enough of it to take a trip to New York and talk to the ABC network people about our doing a kind of Bob and Ray show. The network had lost all the good entertainment programs to television, so they had some time to fill. They gave us a fifteen-minute slot in the evening that was billed as *Frank and Jackson*. Not many people remember this show—it doesn't appear in the anthologies of radio programs, but it ran on a sustaining basis for eighteen months. I did a lot of writing for the show—sketches and other material—and Jackson began reviving some of the voice characters that he had first used in Erie, Pennsylvania. It was really the *Harden and Weaver* show in its embryonic stages, and even when it was dropped, by then we were convinced that we could work together and that there might be a future in the program.

It was around this period that Jackson and I appeared on television together for the first time. Milton Q. Ford had a local show on WMAL-TV that went on after the late news and usually lasted until it ran out of material. We did blackout sketches for that show. Again, it was a way of learning more about each other—trying to achieve a kind of teamwork. The important thing is that we began to realize that we had an on-the-air chemistry, and that it was a basis on which we could build.

One of our memorable one-time TV shows came about by accident. Channel 7 had an afternoon program with Jerry and Jimma Strong as the hosts. It was one of those folksy kinds of shows that featured some interviews and Jimmy Smiley playing the organ. Jerry would sing a song each day, and if he screwed it up, Jimmy Smiley would chastise him on the air. Jerry was either Bing Crosby or Arthur Godfrey—depending on how he felt that day. Jimma had a southern accent, which was part of the down-home charm of the show. She also had a dog on the show to go along with this approach.

One day Jerry and Jimma had to go out of town and they asked Jackson to host the show for that day. It had snowed overnight, and when I left my house in the morning, I noticed that my dog—a real mangy animal—was outside. I didn't have time to mess with him, so I just picked him up and threw him in the car and drove to work. When I got there Jackson told me he was doing *The Jerry and Jimma Show* that day, and he asked me to appear on it with him. I don't know who thought of the scenario, but we decided he would be Jerry and I would be Jimma. I borrowed a fur coat from Dorothy Jones—one of my co-workers—and I went next door to Best & Company and borrowed a wig from one of their mannequins, and we proceeded to do a takeoff on *The Jerry and Jimma Show*. I even had this ratty dog under my arm to complete the picture.

The show was really off the wall, and as it went along people started drifting into the studio from the offices. It wasn't long before the whole station was there watching the goings-on. The sponsor was also there that day, and he was laughing so hard we thought they were going to have to send for the rescue squad. What we didn't know was that Jerry and Jimma had arrived at Union Station, but because of the snow their train had been delayed. They were sitting in the

Savarin Restaurant watching the program on TV. As you might expect, they didn't find what we were doing at all amusing. When they finally returned they told us in no uncertain terms that the sponsor was very upset and that our antics would in all likelihood cost the station the account. Anyhow, Jackson gave Jerry a bill for $30, saying half of that should go to me. Jerry balked at that. He said he had asked only Jack to do the show and that my appearance was Jack's problem. So Jackson revised his bill to $30 for his appearance alone, then split it with me anyway.

While I'm on the subject of television shows, one of the all-time greats on WMAL-TV involved neither Jackson nor me, but was the talk of the station for years afterward.

We had an announcer by the name of Tom Willette—a "big ole boy" from Tennessee who was the MC of a children's program—the usual live fill-in for in between the cartoons. Tom was very resourceful. If he felt something in the news was of particular interest to children, he'd do something on the air about it. Maybe he'd show some drawings or pictures from the newspaper, or maybe conduct an interview.

One day Tom saw an article in the newspaper about a lady visiting Washington who owned a monkey that had been fitted for eyeglasses. The monkey had some kind of an eye problem, and there in the newspaper was a picture of the monkey with his eyeglasses. Tom was smart enough to know that a child was sure to find that amusing or educational or both, so he arranged to have the woman bring the monkey for an appearance on a Saturday morning show. It was winter and there was snow on the ground, but she showed up on schedule with the monkey. Tom was very busy, cueing things and doing live commercials and what-have-you, so the production assistants got the woman all lined up for the interview. She had put the monkey in a little bassinet. Tom had had no time to talk things over with her in advance, but that was the way live television was in those days. So he moved over to the lady and said something like "And now we have a real special visitor," and he started interviewing her. But after taking one look at the monkey, who had been on camera all the while, Tom called for a film commercial, grabbed a headset from a production assistant and told the director, "Don't you realize the damn monkey is dead?" The director found that hard to believe, but Tom kept insisting that the monkey was stone-cold dead—glasses and all. And he was right! The show was live, but the monkey wasn't. He got back to the lady, cut the interview short, and as soon as there was a break, he asked her why in heaven's name she had seen fit to bring a dead monkey on the show. She told him she knew the monkey's appearance had been promoted and didn't want to disappoint the children. Furthermore, she said the monkey had died because of her trip to the station in the bad weather, and as a consequence, she was suing the station. It wasn't long before the general manager issued a memo that under the circumstances became a classic in its own right. It read: "From this date forward, there will be no more live animals on WMAL-TV."

The family that owned the *Evening Star* and the WMAL broadcasting complex were the Kauffmanns, who were very much wrapped up in civic affairs. One of their favorite charities was the Society for Crippled Children. Once in the early fifties, the society kicked off its annual Easter Seal Fund drive with a big television show. The format was of an actual school where the children and their therapists would do a kind of "show and tell." The idea was to show citizens where their money was going. The society brought a group of children who sat around in individual areas with their speech or occupational therapists. They would demonstrate what went on each day in the Crippled Children's Center. I acted as a roving MC, wandering from group to group with my microphone, doing interviews.

At one point I got to a physical therapist—a Swedish lady.

The children were sitting around her, and I began to question her about what she was doing. She was very animated and said, "We're doing very well at our table—for example, little Mary over there has only been here since September and already we've taught her how to screw." I looked at the floor for a while, bit my lip and tried to come up with something to dismiss what she had said, when she spoke up again and offered, "And furthermore, before graduation time she'll know some real fancy screwing." Well, there was no way I could say, "Well, what she means, folks, is . . ." That would just make things worse. What she *did* mean was that the children had certain exercises, one of which involved a big stove bolt. It was threaded and had a nut that screwed onto the bolt. The child had learned to do that motion. But there was no way I could get that across. And I know the Kauffmann family was watching this whole performance from the control room.

What I did was end that segment in a great big hurry and move on to the next therapist hoping for better times. But when the show was over I went to every member of the production crew and thanked them, because if there had been one snicker, it would have brought my career to a screeching halt.

As a booth announcer on TV, you are often called upon to fill in if for some reason the regular talent doesn't make it to the studio. One time Morrie Siegel—who was the regular sports guy—didn't make it for some reason or another, and I was drafted as the pinch hitter. All I had to do was read what somebody else wrote, so there was no problem. Except when it came time for the baseball scores. They weren't in my script because they were being updated on a big board with raised letters as they came in. I was supposed to look up and read them from the board. Big problem: I had worn sunglasses to work that day and I didn't want to wear them on the air, so I was winging it with my bare eyes. When I turned to the board I saw absolutely nothing, squinted, still saw nothing, and finally said, "The scores today involve a lot of different numbers, some of which appear to be fives. My time is up, I thank you for yours."

Meantime back in radio, Bill Malone had succeeded Jimmy Gibbons on the morning show, but just as Gibbons had spent much of his time in sports, Malone was getting a lot of network television assignments and finally decided to give up the daily radio show. When Jackson and I heard Malone was leaving, we thought this would be a good chance to sell management on the idea of reviving the old *Frank and Jackson* show.

I think the first time the top boss really had become aware of our possibilities as a team came in the fall of 1959. The station was playing host to our national representatives—the people who sell us to the agencies in New York—and for some reason or another Jackson and I were chosen to be the entertainment at the station presentation. We did several blackout-type sketches and some generally wild stuff, and they all must have thought it was pretty funny because they were falling all over themselves and we were a big hit.

Around this time a very fortuitous management shuffle happened as well. Andy Ockershausen, who had been national sales manager for both radio and television, was made station manager at WMAL-Radio on February 1, 1960. But he had been negotiating for the job for several months before that—including the period of the presentation for the national reps. It was obvious to Andy that the first step toward getting the station out of the hole it was in would be by strengthening the morning show. He was all for giving Jackson and me a shot at it.

The boss, Fred Houwink, listened to an audition tape we had made and then had all the managers of the other departments hear it and offer their comments. He also told us to write a letter telling him why we should become the new morning men. Actually he didn't have too much to lose. The station was doing so poorly as far as listenership was concerned it owed points to the rating service. Our selling point was that we felt Washington was ready for a team. New York had taken well to Rayburn and Finch, and we figured Harden and Weaver could do a show like that in Washington. Houwink had been exploring other possibilities—he had even considered trying for Jack Paar, among others. But after a lot of thrashing around we were offered a thirteen-week contract. He wasn't taking very many chances. But we had a clause in the contract to the effect that if the *Harden and Weaver* show didn't work out we would get our staff jobs back and we would not lose our seniority. And do you know what? That clause has never been removed from all of our subsequent contracts.

And it was with that show of confidence on both sides that the *Harden and Weaver* show (we had opted for "Harden and Weaver" over the old "Frank and Jackson"—again, not unmindful of Rayburn and Finch in New York) was to be launched in March 1960.

But first we had a big meeting. Nothing ever happens in radio without one. The idea of this meeting was to come up with some kind of promotional campaign with which to launch the program. Members of our advertising agency were there, the program director, the promotion department—all kinds of people. And out of this gathering of the station's best came suggestions for an advertising campaign that may have been some of the worst ideas promulgated at a gathering of its kind in the business. Would you believe someone suggested the slogan "Angels with Tarnished Wings on Cloud 63"? They wanted to build a Styrofoam cloud around an automobile and have us ride all over town in it. Another idea the geniuses came up with was to have two puppets—one a likeness of Harden and the other of Weaver. Announcer Pete Jamerson, who already had a puppet show, would operate the puppets on his TV show. Here they had the real Harden and Weaver and they wanted to use puppets in a promotional campaign.

When all these gems were exhausted I took out some promotional spots that I had written, which made use of Jackson's voices, and they let us go ahead with them. We also filmed a similar spot for television and hired a photographer to take a picture of us on a bicycle built for two—and that was that for the promotion campaign.

Our very first program, as did so many afterward, originated from the WMAL transmitter building on Greentree Road in Bethesda, Maryland. All of our disk jockey shows were done from out there in the countryside. The station had put up a brick building that looked more like a house than a radio station—I guess so it would blend more with what was really a residential area. Greentree Road ended right there, so you didn't travel that part of the road unless your destination was the radio station or you were hopelessly lost. Radio programming occupied the basement. On the main floor the key space was occupied by the transmitter. In the back was the larger of two studios from which the DJ shows were broadcast. The news department, which served both radio and television, consisted of only four people, and the news on the *Harden and Weaver* show was done from the transmitter site. For the remainder of the day, the originating point for news was the combined radio-TV facility on Connecticut Avenue. Our first newsman, Len Deibert, had a tiny room with an AP news wire clattering away at the transmitter site.

Harden and Weaver's debut certainly was the most insignificant of many changes that would take place in Washington in the months ahead. Before long, John F. Kennedy would be launching his New Frontier. The city would be awakening from a sleep. There was a great deal of excitement. The "Best and the Brightest," as David Halberstam would characterize them, would be gathering in the city. We would have competition for Washington's attention in the first couple of years.

We arrived at the station early. I had already chosen the music and written some bits that would feature Jackson's voice characterizations, and the show moved along without any serious glitches. We had worked together enough in the past to be fairly comfortable with each other. I don't think that first show will be included in any anthology of radio's greatest local programs. But I don't believe it was among the worst, either. During the show we received a number of encouraging telephone calls from listeners, but that's the usual routine. You'll always find some kind souls out there no matter how bad you are. But the strange thing was that not one of our colleagues called from the downtown offices. We had expected some verdict from members of the staff—but no one had called when we got off the air at nine. Then at around 11:15, the phone rang off the hook. Everybody called to tell us how well they felt the show had gone. Later we found out the reason for this two-hour gap. Fred Houwink had not come into the office until 11:15, and obviously everyone was waiting to hear his reaction to the show before they were going to commit themselves.

The station did a rather unusual thing in promoting the *Harden and Weaver* show—not in our market but in New York, where the agencies that bought national spots were located. They purchased fifteen minutes of time on WVNJ in the New York metropolitan area to explain to the account executives there what WMAL in Washington was doing now. Jackson and I did some routines for that show—it was all taped—and it went on the air at 10:30 in the morning when most of the agency people would be in their offices and could tune in. Word went out that the program would be on at that time. I don't know if it sold any national spots for Harden and Weaver, but in those days it was rather unusual for a radio station in one market to be buying time on a radio station in another market.

And so it began. But the *Harden and Weaver* show did not take Washington by storm. We were starting from ground zero. We had only four regularly scheduled one-minute commercials when we launched the show that first day. Two of those brave companies—Northwest Orient Airlines and Citizens' Bank of Maryland—were there at the creation and never left us. Although it took a while to build an audience, sponsors began to get interested almost immediately.

In those days it was pretty much Harden and Weaver period. We picked our own music, answered the telephones, did our own correspondence. It was as if management had said, "Go get 'em, Rover!" and turned its attention to more important matters.

But we felt that was a plus. We'd get our own ideas for promotions, and just about all the input on the program was from Harden and Weaver. I think the most affirmative contribution from management was the decision not to interfere. It helped us to find our own way—to establish the personality of the show.

At the outset we began getting requests for public appearances, and we realized how important these could be in building recognition in the market. We went everywhere—little clubs, big organizations—if as many as four people could be collected in a room, we'd entertain them. Often we'd go to speak at a luncheon and then at a dinner the same day. Once we completed the circuit of all the civic, business and service clubs, we started all over again. We worked longer hours off the air than on. There is no doubt that these appearances had a great deal to do with whatever success Harden and Weaver were to enjoy.

The listenership began to build and there was an increasingly heavy mail response. And we noticed a willingness of these correspondents to participate, to furnish us with ideas for the show, to involve themselves. We welcomed it with open arms. It simply reinforced the hope we had from the start—that there was a potential audience out there that would identify with two people who were quite ordinary but who didn't mind breaking some of the so-called rules of broadcasting. We don't worry about dead air like so many people do in this business. The main theme of the *Harden and Weaver* show is its "laid-back" approach. You'll hear us say time and time again on the air, "One of these days we've got to do it like it's supposed to be done." Of course, we never will. We're not that stupid. You change a horse's pace and he loses the race.

I think you can define us best by what we are not. We are not zany. Jackson is not Pinky Lee. Though he takes on a number of characters, they are just that—characters, not caricatures. No matter who is saying what, it's something you're apt to hear from somebody you know. Of course, there are exaggerations, but we try to be believable. Jackson steps out of his many roles on occasion to be serious when the situation calls for it. I can be a bit caustic every once in a while—but it's usually on behalf of Everyman railing against the system. We don't pose as heavyweights. We shy away from controversy, and you won't hear us taking stands on the burning issues of the day. We'll acknowledge an issue—satirically—but we won't climb on any soapbox. To tell you the truth, I think our opinions are irrelevant. If you want controversy try the talk shows. We're not in the business of alienating people.

In the beginning we scripted some bits of the show, but once we got rolling it became strictly ad-lib. I guess the thing people began talking about most was our treatment of the commercials. We'd use them as program content—going off on long digressions (which would get us in trouble with the FCC later) and generally hoking things up. We were by no means the first to take a lighthearted, irreverent approach to commercials, but it became a big part of our act. And Jackson would create these marvelous imaginary characters. For instance, there was Rocky Rockmont. The sponsor was Rockmont Chevrolet, so Jackson came up with a rough-talking character who was supposedly the owner of the firm. This had not been planned in advance. We were doing the commercial one morning, and I turned the page and said, "As Oglethorpe Rocky Rockmont says," and I pointed to Jackson, knowing he would come up with something. What he came up with was this gruff-voiced character, and Rocky was born there and then—a bit illegitimately, I suppose, because of course there was no such person. As a matter of fact, the time came when we met the owner of Rockmont Chevrolet—Frank Williams—and he came across like an Ivy Leaguer, absolutely the opposite of Rocky. Rocky was a diamond in the rough and he never got any respect. The Rockmont Chevrolet spot became an entertainment feature. Apparently it was doing a pretty good job because when we visited the sponsor almost six months after the account started we were told, "Whatever it is that you're doing—please keep it up." Their salespeople all wore "Rocky" buttons. People came into Rockmont Chevrolet saying they wanted to buy their cars from Rocky personally. This went on for six or seven years, which is about as long as you can stretch a gimmick like that. Then the company went another route . . . and Rocky was laid to rest.

When you start out as only an asterisk in the ratings book, the climb isn't likely to be meteoric. But we made steady progress until after three or four years it became obvious that the program was a positive success. We were in good enough shape for the station to do the first of the *Harden and Weaver* show anniversary remotes on our fifth birthday in March 1965. The Mediastat rating report for October-November of that year had showed the *Harden and Weaver* program with a Metro Total Persons' share of 18. WRC, which then had Al Ross in the same time period, had a 15.2 rating. WTOP's Eddie Gallaher was third in line with a 12.4 rating. It's interesting to note that all three network stations were featuring middle-of-the-road formats.

After the morning show was set, the station continued to experiment with the other times of day. In the late morning, Jerry and Jimma Strong had been doing a "Mr. and Mrs." kind of program, which gave way to Jerry as a solo performer. Tom Willette got a crack at it next. And then, prompted by the success of the two-man show in the morning, Bill Trumbull and George Wilson teamed up for a time. Afterward came the Jim Evans period. Or periods. Evans may be the only radio performer ever hired three times and fired three times by the same radio station. Jim was a very talented performer who had strong opinions about most things. He was also a musician who wrote satirical songs about the various news stories of the day. Anyone who expressed his convictions the way he did in those days was bound to become controversial, so he kept getting into hot water with management. The fact that they kept rehiring him was proof enough that he was considered a unique talent. Finally in 1968 Tom Gauger moved into that time slot and found a home.

Afternoon drive time was another game of musical chairs for many years. When Harden and Weaver began in the morning, Herb Davis was doing the afternoon show. He was followed by Steve Gilmartin, the sportscaster who gave way to Johnny Wilcox and finally to Bill Trumbull in 1968.

Trumbull has been in that area ever since, later teaming with Ed Meyer for the program called *Two for the Road* and then with Chris Core for *The Trumbull and Core Show*.

The one constant was the evening program where Felix Grant had been purveying jazz since 1954. In the late seventies, the station decided it could no longer afford the luxury of such a specialized show and announced that Felix would henceforth only be heard on weekends. But this announcement kicked up such a storm of protest letters that the station ran up the white flag, even took an ad in the newspaper to admit it had made a mistake. "Old Shoe" was back at his old stand.

The overnight show became the province of Bill Mayhugh in 1964. We join Bill at 5:30 in the morning as sort of a transition to the *Harden and Weaver* program at 6:00. John Lyon has been a tower of strength in every time slot.

It was definitely the early success of the *Harden and Weaver* show in the morning that paved the way for the station to add continually to the product that eventually made it dominant in the market.

In 1960 there were only six newsmen who served both WMAL-Radio and WMAL-TV. Del Malkie was Mr. Local News on television, which was just starting to realize the potential of local newscasts. Three of the newsmen on the staff are still with the station—Len Deibert, Joseph McCaffrey and Ed Meyer. And the remarkable Larry Krebs was roaming the streets of Washington at night, supplying film stories, just as he serves WMAL-Radio to this day.

In September 1963 a traffic helicopter, manned by DC police officers, made its debut on the *Harden and Weaver* show. The helicopter represented a major investment of some $80,000 and was the only "trafficopter" on the East Coast. A second newsperson was added to the morning show so that one person could do the newscasts on the hour and another those on the half hour. The station also turned very sports conscious, becoming the flagship station for the Washington Redskins and adding a sportscaster for morning drive time. And we got our first producer when Connie Adams assumed a variety of duties on the *Harden and Weaver* show in the late sixties.

By the end of the first decade, our show was a sold-out proposition. I'm not sure what the opposition stations were doing at that time, but Johnny Holliday, who joined WWDC from KYA, San Francisco, in 1970 (and who is now with WMAL), told me this story recently:

"When I came to Washington, my bosses told me my major competition would be a two-man team called Harden and Weaver. While I was breaking in, I worked the afternoons for a while, so I had a chance to listen to WMAL in the morning. I was pretty confident after hearing them that it shouldn't take me too long to beat them out. After all, the two stations were doing basically the same thing—both middle-of-the-road stations. We had the helicopter and the heavy emphasis on news and sports, and we had Washington Senators baseball and community involvement. And, as for Jackson Weaver's voices, heck, I had twenty-seven different characters, and I did a lot of speaking engagements outside. I thought it would be just a matter of time before I caught them.

"But it never happened. For seven years I chased after them, but I never caught them. I met Frank and Jack for the first time at some function, and Jackson went out of his way to be nice to me. And after my plane crash accident in 1975, when I returned to work after the long hospitalization, WWDC had sort of a welcome back first broadcast at the Shoreham Hotel . . . and Harden and Weaver had taped a special 'glad you're back' routine that was played on my show. It's no secret that most people who worked in radio in this market thought of WMAL as the place to be.

"For me it was the old 'if you can't beat 'em, join 'em' routine. I first applied at WMAL in 1974, but they had no openings. I finally made it in March of 1979. The Great Harden and Weaver Chase was over for Johnny Holliday."

I would say one of the reasons for the success of the *Harden and Weaver* program is our willingness to emphasize what we think is important to our audience. We converted the show into a source of information long before others in the Washington area caught on to the logic of such a format. We may fool around a lot on the air—but the program can be transformed immediately into an information service.

Some years back a hurricane swept far inland before blowing itself out over Chesapeake Bay, and it caused widespread flooding in the Washington area and on the Eastern Shore. We told our audience that we were wearing our yellow slickers and rain hats and that we were turning our show into a hurricane watch. Along with the station's regular newscasts twice an hour, we used dozens of individual reports from WMAL reporters in the field and from stringers. We simply used the program as a way of funneling necessary information to the audience. In this day of all-news stations that doesn't sound unique, but at the time no one was providing that kind of flexibility.

We were also the first in the area to really emphasize school closings and cancellations on snowstorm days. We called ourselves "Snow Birds" and relayed the information provided by our news department. The station has always prided itself on its comprehensive coverage of every school or organization, no matter how small. One morning while reading what seemed like tons of school cancellations, Jackson tossed in the closing of the Rinky Dinky Day School. There is no such school, but from then on every snow day, if we don't mention whether the Rinky Dinky Day School is open or closed, we'll get several calls from "anxious parents."

Providing information in the Washington area sometimes gets difficult because of the many jurisdictions—some of them overlapping. For instance, an accident on the Woodrow Wilson Bridge could involve either the District of Columbia, Virginia or Maryland, depending on which part of the bridge was the scene of the accident. I remember one day when a water main belonging to the city of Falls Church, Virginia, ruptured under a road in Arlington County, affecting mainly Fairfax County commuters. One of those caught in the traffic jam was Interior Secretary Stewart Udall. When he finally arrived at work hours later, he complained to the District of Columbia Commissioners. Our news department provided me with a blow-by-blow account of this multi-jurisdictional hassle, which I read on the air, involving Falls Church, Arlington, Fairfax County, the Interior Department, the Park Police and the District Commissioners. When I finished, Jackson—in the woman's voice—asked, "Does the United Nations know about this?"

HARDEN AND WEAVER GALLERY

WOMAN: Did you ever wonder, What did Elizabeth Taylor ever do with her Passover dishes?

Jackson: Building Character(s)

I suppose the one thing that lends a certain amount of variety to our show is the cast of characters that has evolved over the years. Some of these characters remained pretty much as I had created them in Erie, Pennsylvania. Some came along as a product of the times and were abandoned when they went out of date. And it takes no genius to know that many of the ideas were lifted from other people or other shows. The senator who leads the march every morning is just another version of Kenny Delmar's Senator Claghorn—although I had a similar character before Claghorn came along. As Frank describes the senator often on the show, "If he can't come up with an equivocation, he always has an ambiguity. He gives a definite maybe to everything." I also give the senator an eye for the ladies. He answers more cocktail calls than quorum calls. Once I was introduced to Lady Bird Johnson, whose husband was then the Senate majority leader, and she told me, "You-all better stop talkin' like that with that senator—people gonna *believe* you."

The most familiar of the characters is the female voice—I use her more than any other. The lady doesn't even have a name, God bless her, but there are people who swear they know what she looks like. People constantly refer to her as "the little old lady"—but I've never described her as little or old or anything else. But the listeners seem to know someone just like her—an aunt back in Peoria who is a little absent-minded, who has an opinion on everything and really doesn't know much about anything. We always have her work in a malapropism—such as referring to the "venereal equinox" or "heat prostitution." It's Frank's role to jump right in and quickly straighten her out.

The "Larry" character is the only impersonation that I do. I guess everybody does a Lawrence Welk. But we always work him in when we play a Lawrence Welk record.

One morning I had been doing the Welk bit and we got a telephone call from National Airport. It was Welk. He had been listening to us on his way to the airport and had decided to give us a call. We put him on the air—with me talking to him, and although I tried to play it straight, I kept finding myself wanting to do my Welk routine. It was such a switch—somebody else talking like Welk instead of me—I felt like I was having a conversation with myself.

Dr. Willoughby is our resident psychiatrist. Frank used to write bits for him when analysis became the thing in the fifties, and this was just a satire on that whole syndrome. Dr. Willoughby usually comes on with no warning—depending upon what we happen to be discussing. Frank may give me no more of a cue than "What do you think of that, Dr. Willoughby?" We usually know right away whether the routine is going to fly or not. If it doesn't seem to be getting anywhere, we simply drop it and go on to something else. That's the beauty of not working with prepared material—you're not committed to it.

Dr. Headcold is our musicologist. We stole him outright from the old Ransom Sherman *Club Matinee*, which goes back to the thirties on the Blue Network. We even stole his description—a professor of music at Albino State Teachers' College across from Goldfarb's Hacienda, overlooking the River Shannon. Albino State's chief rival in football is Abernathy Normal—old Ab Normal. Once a listener wrote us: "You guys—who are you trying to kid? I remember Ransom Sherman and all those guys—I know where you got that Dr. Headcold." But we've never tried to hide our thefts.

There is the voice of an old codger—we've never named him, but most listeners refer to him as the old-timer. *We* don't, because somebody else had a character by that name and, for once, we weren't stealing it. Anyway this old salt, or whatever you want to call him, is sometimes used as the conscience of the listener. He brings up things that Harden and Weaver are too chicken to touch. He is usually in violent disagreement with the woman and makes no bones about his disgust with some of her comments. He's always putting her down and we are forced to step in and mediate the dispute. The old guy has a very conservative bent—he is out of step with the modern world and its permissiveness.

Bosco Osgood is somewhat akin to a character created by Bob and Ray—a reporter in the field. Actually he's supposed to do a remote broadcast, but he never arrives at the right place. If Bosco's supposed to report on the Super Bowl from Detroit—somehow or other he ends up in Miami. His routine never changes. He's always running into a girl who needs help. The girl is obviously taking advantage of him, but he sees her only as "this sweet young thing." He's spent all his money on her and he needs more. Bosco is a loser. While other sportscasters travel first-class, we make Bosco answer want ads for rides. He has to get his tickets to the events he covers from the USO. The bit always ends the same way—with Bosco on the telephone pleading for more money and fighting an unsuccessful battle to keep Frank from hanging up.

One character we used to use quite a bit in the early days was Chuck Roast. Chuck had a hint of mint—maybe even more than a hint, but this was before the closet doors were thrown open. Chuck was nothing more than a Franklin Pangborn kind of character, but we had to stop having those barbecues in Georgetown with Chuck Roast presiding, because nowadays some activist group might be up here protesting.

Once we had a character who was based on our boss at the time, but who really represented the comptroller of any organization. Dudley Stokes would put up signs like "Remember, better programs come from clean studios." He was always turning out the lights to save money. Dudley could see no reason for a full string section in a symphony orchestra. The only thing he could read was the bottom line. Just about everyone has had an experience with a penny-pinching boss. We'd just drop Dudley in every once in a while.

Phil Dirt is our garden editor. He's a character based on an incongruity: a tough guy with a New York accent talking about flowers and plants. He usually substitutes for Pete Moss.

We had a teenager who was rather like Henry Aldrich, and a poet by the name of Percy Dovebreath who was a steal from the late Ernie Kovacs's Percy Dovetonsils—but we never used them much.

Then there are a number of nameless throw-in characters I do just to make use of my dialects. I do two kinds of British accent as well as Australian, Italian, Swedish, Scots, Irish, Spanish, Chicano, Russian and Yiddish. We have to be more careful now. People have become more sensitive about ethnicity. Television plunges right into those areas. But we definitely react when we get calls from people who are unhappy. It's certainly not our plan to offend anyone.

There has actually been a spinoff from Bosco Osgood on the show. We had done the bit any number of times when a letter arrived—purporting to be from a girl named Pamela. She accused Harden and Weaver of trying to break up her close association with Bosco, and generally took us to task for what she considered our rather cavalier treatment of this noble fellow. Of course, we read Pamela's letter on the air. Several weeks later another letter from Pamela arrived—again chastising us for interfering in what she described as her close relationship with Bosco. That set the pattern for what became a one-way correspondence from Pamela, which continues to this day. The letters have come from all over the world—leading us to the conclusion that Pamela is either an airline stewardess or spends all of her time traveling. Listeners respond in many different ways—trying to join the fun. So we've also received some phony Pamela letters talking about Bosco. We know they are phony, because the "real" Pamela has a particular style that's easy to pick out. But the whole thing is a little unusual. Here we create a character who doesn't exist. Someone else creates a character to keep him company. Then people make believe they are the make-believe characters.

You never know how some people are going to react. One day I got a phone call from a man who was outraged by the fact that I was using the woman's voice. He said I was encouraging homosexuality.

We also had a manager who wanted us to either kill the woman off or tone her down at least. He thought she would be offensive to the women's libbers. To me this was like asking Bjorn Borg to take the strings off his racket. Of course the lady stayed.

Frank: Senator, Are We Ready to March?

In any market look for the dominant station and you will usually see that it is a twenty-four-hour station and that it has the top-rated morning show. The other things will usually fall into line.

At the time Harden and Weaver set sail for their thirteen weeks, the owners of the station were ready to unload it. They had moved most of the operation from the Connecticut Avenue radio-TV complex to the transmitter site in Bethesda so that the radio portion could be a separate unit and could be sold that way. I would venture to guess that unless they were given some slight hope that the station's poor position in the market could be turned around, the owners were prepared to dump it. Harden and Weaver's mild success in the early days may have offered that flicker of hope. At any rate the owners kept the station, and some fifteen years later when the station had to be sold because of FCC divestiture rules, it brought the highest price for any radio station in the history of the industry up to that time.

How much did Harden and Weaver contribute to its success? Comedian Mark Russell, in his act at the Shoreham Hotel, said ABC dropped $16 million in the city of Washington—$15,999,999 for Harden and Weaver, and $1 for WMAL! One of the vice-presidents of ABC used the same line when he visited the station.

The performers at WMAL get fantastic, unparalleled support. The news effort, the sales effort—every aspect of the station—make it a model for the industry. Qualitatively and quantitatively we get more support than any program on the air. However, it wasn't there at the start, it came after we were successful. To be shamelessly immodest, the *Harden and Weaver* show gave the station the toehold it needed—we provided the foundation on which it could build.

How did we do that? You tell us. You could take two guys and have them do exactly the same thing—you could work everything out on a computer and it still wouldn't sound the same. Maybe it has to do with chemistry or metabolism. It's definitely a symbiotic relationship that we have toward each other on the air. We don't do anything outstanding. As a matter of fact, there's a great deal of repetition on our program. People ask, "How do you think of all those things to say?" When I rack my brain to come up with one unusual thing that we said or did, I have to conclude that we didn't. It certainly isn't the music we use. A phonograph record doesn't sound any different on 630 kilocycles than anywhere else on the band. We come across like two ordinary people who think about the same things that occupy the thoughts of the average Washington-area citizen. We are not sequin-encrusted, tinseled show people—we're just people, period. We try to present something with which an audience can identify. Our listeners are very loyal to us. Many tell us that sometimes they get a little tired of us and wander off to try some other station, but they come back finally, and it's like they've returned home. The whole radio station has that loyalty. People tell us they like us simply because we seem interested in each other and we get along so well. I think people pick up the spirit of what we're doing because we do it naturally. It's not as if some consultant had set up a kind of forced chitchat between the anchorman and the sports person.

That's phony and you can't hide that phoniness, that staged camaraderie.

Our audience stays with us also because we are all creatures of habit. Why do you always take a certain route when you go somewhere? You do it because if offers the least resistance or because it's the most pleasant way to go.

There is also the credibility factor. Our listeners are convinced that we will not knowingly steer them wrong. The credibility factor is especially strong in our information service—our news department.

According to the demographics, the Harden and Weaver audience is said to be adult—with little appeal to the young. Yet this act has been invited by just about every high school in the area to address graduation ceremonies. And the invitations come from the students, not the school officials or parents. We don't accept invitations to graduations because we feel a couple of clowns would not be appropriate on such occasions. But we *do* appear before student groups time and again. On one occasion, the students were studying about Egypt. They knew we had just been there and wanted us to tell them about that country. We had only been there for three days and weren't about to pose as experts on the subject. But from the way the young people phrased their questions, it was obvious they had listened to our program.

Are we oriented only to the suburbs? Get into any metropolitan taxi and check on the driver's listening habits. One person called to tell us the family had moved here only recently and had learned about the whole area by listening to us talk about every flea market and bazaar in every community.

Once a foreign waiter came up to Jackson in a restaurant and told him he had learned to speak English by listening to us talk so much.

You'd be surprised at the number of people who call us to talk about intimate personal matters, as though they were speaking to their family physician or clergyman. They want us to help settle domestic quarrels . . . or help name the baby. Some have even called threatening suicide, and we became a suicide hotline. I guess the vast number of lonely people out there accounts for the popularity of soap operas.

Many people call us with questions, but they're not really seeking answers—they just want to talk to somebody. We suddenly become their pals. I can't understand radio stations that actually block calls, that won't give out telephone numbers. Radio may be a mass medium, but I don't think you should lose sight of the fact that the mass is made up of individuals. It's still one on one, and when you've forgotten that, you've lost the ballgame.

And through all this, after all these years most people don't know which one is Harden and which one is Weaver and who does what. When they guess they are usually wrong. One of our clients, who owns a Chinese restaurant, has very animated conversations with us through which I can detect that he thinks Harden and Weaver are one person. Even with the two of us standing there. He thinks one of us is the agent.

Unlike many broadcasters who keep their ears tuned to the industry, we like to muddle along in complete oblivion. We don't pay any attention to what anyone else is doing. This is not some form of elitism. I just have the idea that if you pay too much attention to what others are doing, you may begin to react to it. I've never heard our competition in the morning. First of all, you can't do much listening when you're on the air at the same time—but neither do we have the other programs taped for us. We just do our thing and let them do their thing. As long as what we're doing seems to be working, why should we take a chance on hobbling a winning horse?

Some broadcasters wonder how two old-timers can continue to attract an audience with what we do. They say we break all the rules of good broadcasting. Well, who makes the rules? It seems to us if there are any rules, they would be simply to put on a program that people want to listen to—and that sponsors think will sell their products or services. If you use those rules as a yardstick, we can't be too far off the pace.

I guess that's why we get so stubborn when the programming department tries to make the music on the *Harden and Weaver* program conform to some kind of formula that they've devised for the rest of the shows. Those are really the only attempts that have ever been made to change what we do. Of course, the whole thing is a little ridiculous when you consider how few records we can squeeze into the program. Apparently programmers have meetings, or check with consultants from time to time, and decide that certain records should be played at such and such a time because they're big records in the industry or something. We try to explain that you could play bugle calls on the show and it wouldn't make any difference. The program is predicated on the personalities of Harden and Weaver, so the music is necessarily an extension of those personalities. So my feeling is, don't come to me and say, "Do not play a Beatles record," anymore than you would say, "You *must* play a Neil Sedaka record." That's ridiculous on both counts.

If you try to explain our program on the basis of what's happening in the industry, you might as well check into the funny farm. For example, what would one of those high-priced consultants say if you told him you had a morning radio show in a major market with a rather sophisticated audience, and that you played a hymn at a certain time during the rush hour and a march, also at the same time every morning. He would tell you, between giggles, that there is no way you can get away with that. Well, not only have we been getting away with it for twenty years, but we couldn't change it if we wanted to. The listeners would attack the station. We catch it if for some reason those features are delayed beyond their regular time. And when we're on vacation—John

Lyon, or someone else who may be sitting in, will do his own thing—except he'll play the hymn and the march just to avoid some nasty phone calls.

But every so often the new music formula is launched—and Harden and Weaver are asked to conform. Once it even got to the point where certain records were hidden so we couldn't play them. It's our contention that if someone wants to play radio station, there's plenty of time to do it after 10:00 A.M.

Getting back to consultants—they come in and survey your station to see what you're doing, then they take polls in your listening area to see which personalities in the market get a positive response. They've got a noninventory commodity to sell and will come up with a list of recommendations on what you must do to increase your audience and thereby boost your sales. I always figure an expert is someone with a briefcase who is more than twelve miles from where he lives.

Now I have to say that consultants probably have profited some stations. They see nothing wrong with having a carbon copy of a station in every locality just like having a McDonald's Restaurant everywhere. I just don't believe, however, that just because something works in Hastings, Nebraska, that it's going to work in Washington. Supposedly they lean heavily on their surveys of the particular market to find out what will play there. They leaned heavily on surveys before they built the Edsel, too.

Look at local television news programs if you want to see how the consultants gave us Tweedledum and Tweedledee. All the anchorpeople look as if they were produced by a cookie cutter. And they all perform their happy talk with the sports guy or the weather person; and the shows all feature reporters who bring you investigative stories on teenage sex or male go-go dancers or whatever else they can out-titillate each other with on that particular night.

We've been told that programming executives from other big stations have come to town to find out what this Harden and Weaver business is all about. They hole up in a hotel and listen to us for a week, and they're kind of amazed at how easy it all is. And they go back to Cincinnati and get Charlie and Fred and say, "Hey—Harden and Weaver don't do much of anything and they're big stuff. You guys can do that—you give the weather and the time and make some inane statement and read a lot of public service announcements. Hell, you can do that—you're our new tandem team—it's the Charlie and Fred Show!" But it doesn't work because there's a little bit more to it than that. It's a matter of the proper chemistry. Maybe Charlie and Fred just aren't the right mix. Maybe they don't even like each other all that much. Maybe there's something different between Cincinnati and Washington. The difference, whatever it is, may be almost imperceptible. But it's there. And so it doesn't work.

As we did the show, a certain division of duties developed. We never sat down and said, "Frank will do this and Jackson will do that." But I had been doing the morning show for a while before we teamed up, so it was natural that I would continue to devise the music sheets and to take care of the log. Jackson handled all the telephone calls—not because he liked talking on the phone, but because his seat happened to be nearest the phone. How do you like that for good planning? In the early days I used to write some sketches for us, since we had a lot of time and very few commercials. But we simply don't have the time to spare on the air anymore for much fooling around. Management might consider this a cop-out, but our chief function on the program is to make the commercials palatable. Not long ago we appeared at a luncheon and, as usual, we did a little routine about our job description. A person in the audience popped up and said, "I know what your job is. It's to separate the commercials!" And there's a lot of truth to that. Not that it's an easy job to accommodate the commercials on our schedule. It's a little disheartening to look up at the clock and see that you have eight minutes left, and you still have five commercials to squeeze in plus other business to take care of. How do you separate those commercials gracefully? That's our job.

HARDEN AND WEAVER GALLERY

FRANK: Senator, if the President's budget were to come up for a vote on the floor tomorrow, would you be for it or against it?

SENATOR: Well, let me say this about that. You have asked a question that's in the minds of most of the American people today. And we must always think of it in that context. For you see we are in . . .

FRANK: Perhaps I can rephrase the question.

SENATOR: You might do that.

FRANK: In the event the administration's budget were to come up for a rollcall vote . . .

SENATOR: Up yonder?

FRANK: No, right here in the Senate.

SENATOR: Oh, I see.

FRANK: Would you vote yea or nay?

SENATOR: The answer to that question has echoed in the hallowed halls of Congress for hundreds of years. Yea or nay. I would vote consistent with my commitments from the rockbound shores of Maine to the white sands of New Mexico. I'll always stand on my record, as shaky as it is . . .

FRANK: Thank you, Senator.

Jackson: "You Win Some, and . . ."

Of the thousands of commercial accounts that we have butchered on the air, we've only managed to lose two sponsors . . . and they eventually came back with us. It may not be a secret that we read all of our commercials cold. So if it's a new commercial, Harden and Weaver and their listeners are becoming acquainted with it together. That's not how you're taught to do it. You're supposed to go over the copy to make sure there are no typos and maybe read it a few times so you can do a decent selling job. But we just don't have the time. And besides, if we sounded smooth, like other announcers, people would think we're playing radio. It just wouldn't be us if everything went the way the agency thought it would when they wrote the copy.

Well, one day back in the sixties we did a spot for the Julius Garfinckel Company—a large local department store. Their commercials would occasionally call attention to some event that was going to take place at one of the branch stores. That day's spot let people know that a famous fashion designer by the name of Irving Baer was going to be at one of the stores. As expected, this provoked us to wonder if perhaps Mama Baer and the Three Little Baers were going to be there, too. It wasn't very funny, but suddenly I came up with one of my transpositions—calling the store Garlius Jewlfinkel, which started us laughing so much we couldn't finish the spot. We just signaled the engineer to play a record so we could regroup. While the record was playing, we decided that we had done such a dismal job—we never really got the name of the store right or the address or any of the key information—that we would start all over again and do it properly without any fooling around. To make sure of that, Frank walked out and left the job to me. He was afraid he might break up on the air again. So the record ended and I launched into the spot—doing it straight—and everything went well until I got to the tag line, which went something like ". . . and you can see it at Garfinckel's." For some reason, I said, "And you can see it at all Hecht Company stores." I have no idea why I said that. Garfinckel's certainly had no idea why I said it. They called up and cancelled the spot. But they proved to have a forgiving nature and eventually came back.

The other account we lost was the *Washington Evening Star*. This was unusual, since the *Star* owned WMAL. If we couldn't make them happy, they should have cancelled us altogether instead of just their commercial. They dropped us because they didn't like the fact that we took some liberties with the copy—something the other sponsors were begging us to do. Much later when there were new owners of the *Star*, they gave us some very funny agency-produced commercials featuring Sam and Janet Evening that were a lot crazier than anything we had done earlier.

I think most of our clients are aware that we never make fun of a sponsor or the product. The thing that we play around with is simply the very fact of a radio commercial itself.

Though we normally steer clear of controversy, we have on occasion embraced a cause or two and have run up some remarkable failures. There was the time we found out that the Air Force was going to do away with the band's bagpipe group known as the Pipes. I think the wife of some general didn't think it was very manly for some of the men to be dressing up in kilts. They decided to do away with this band feature. So we got on the air to do battle in favor of saving the Pipes, and we got a lot of favorable response from listeners, but the Air Force went right ahead and abolished the band, anyway. Obviously the general's wife had a lot more clout than Harden and Weaver.

There was also the time we tried to save the Watergate Barge as the setting for military band concerts. The bands used to perform on a barge moored on the Potomac River right behind the Lincoln Memorial. It was a pleasant setting, and on summer nights people would gather across the roadway to listen under the stars. Boaters would anchor nearby in the river for the same purpose. True, it was in the flight path of aircraft coming in and out of National Airport and things got noisy on occasion, but that was only a minor impediment to the evening's entertainment. One day the Watergate Barge (which was so named before the Watergate apartments were built, and predated the time when Watergate would mean something else) sprang a leak (which could not be fixed by the Nixon Plumbers), and the Park Service decided to abandon ship. We came to the conclusion that the Watergate Barge had to be saved and even came up with a list of barges that might be available to take the place of the leaky one. Again, we found a great deal of support among the citizens, but absolutely none where it really counted. The idea was dropped. The concerts continued—on the steps of the Capitol Building, at the Jefferson Memorial and in other quite satisfactory settings—and it became obvious that our campaign had more holes in it than the barge.

One time I went to Baltimore to see the ship *Constellation*, which had been neglected and was in pretty bad shape. When I came back we discussed this on the air—

how the sister ship of the *Constitution* was being treated so badly and all. I made the suggestion that maybe the ship should be taken to Annapolis and made into a museum. A member of the Maryland House of Delegates got wind of this, thought it was a great idea and immediately introduced a bill to that effect. We talked it up on the air, and were feeling pretty pleased with ourselves for coming to the rescue of the poor *Constellation*, when one day the phone rang. The caller was Arleigh Burke—the former Chief of Naval Operations. He was enraged. He said a private foundation was hard at work on the refitting and preserving of the ship and suggested that we bug off before we manage to blow the whole deal. It was a little embarrassing, especially since the Maryland legislator hadn't checked into the situation before he jumped right in and dropped the bill in the hopper. The *Constellation*, no thanks to us, is now in good shape—still in Baltimore and a popular feature of that city's Harborplace waterfront redevelopment.

We made a better choice for a cause when we came to the defense of the *Savannah*—the nation's first nuclear-powered merchant ship. I had read that about five hundred ship's captains had signed a petition, urging that the vessel be saved from the scrap heap. We talked about this, quoting from an article in the newspaper. A listener happened to be Georgia Congressman Elliot Hagan, who called to tell us that a congressional committee was meeting that very day on the subject of saving the *Savannah*. He was later to credit us with gaining a one-year reprieve for the ship. Hagan arranged for us to go abroad and also took us to a meeting of the Savannah City Council, where he talked about Harden and Weaver to a puzzled group of council members who didn't have the slightest notion of who the two strange birds were that the congressman had hauled before them.

Congressman Hagan had become our friend a long time

before that episode. One day on the show, Frank had mentioned the town of Ludowici, Georgia. The phone rang immediately. It was Hagan who said, "All I want to know is how you two clowns ever heard of Ludowici, Georgia." He invited us to lunch and became a friend of the *Harden and Weaver* program. Of course, Frank's association with and affection for the city of Savannah would come up from time to time on our program, and one time we were invited to participate in Founders' Day ceremonies in Savannah. The big doings took place on the steps of City Hall. Among those participating was Governor Jimmy Carter, who made me an honorary citizen of Georgia.

Standing on the steps, we were about a half block away from a cannon that had been donated to the city by General George Washington way back when. The cannon is fired on every Founders' Day, and I guess the mayor, John Rousakas, didn't exactly know the schedule of events. He got up to make his speech and managed to say, "Ladies and gentlemen . . ." when there was a tremendous explosion of the cannon. The mayor, nonplussed, continued, "Now that I have your attention . . ."

Presently the honored guests got into a "coach-and-four" for the big parade. About halfway down the parade route, Governor Carter jumped out and walked the rest of the way. I guess it was a warm-up for a similar kind of walk—along Pennsylvania Avenue during his inauguration as President some years later.

We stuck our noses in another matter involving the U.S. Navy, and it may be that we scored a victory.

Almost every year we are called upon to MC the Navy League's annual dinner. The affair involves some twenty-five hundred people—high Navy brass and Navy suppliers in the military-industrial complex. We participated one year when the Navy Band was under the direction of Lieutenant Anthony Mitchell. It occurred to us that the leaders of all the other military bands were full colonels. So we chose that forum to point out what we thought was an obvious oversight—that Lieutenant Mitchell was not being treated with the proper respect. Then we went back and continued the subject on the air for several days—knocking the Navy for its lack of comparability. Mitchell was promoted within two months. He claims we did it, but it may well be that the promotion already was in the mill. At least we didn't get him demoted.

One more Navy story. One day we were at an event, sitting on the dais with Navy Secretary John Chaffee, when a band started performing. The music was, well, ear shattering, and the secretary said, "What the hell is that?" I didn't quite know how to inform him that the group was one of the units of the Navy Band—a rock group. The members weren't performing in their naval uniforms, but they belonged to his Navy. I just changed the subject real fast.

Frank: The Feeling Is Mutual

The best way to judge the effectiveness of a radio program or a station is by the degree of listener response. Our audience always wants to be involved with what's on the air. One time we read a letter from a listener and it happened to include a pun. So then other people started sending us puns. It got to the point where we were receiving sixty puns a day. Some listener would write, "Now I know you haven't heard this one because I just made it up!" But not only would it be a pun that was forty-two years old, it was one we had already used two or three times on the air. We finally had to stop reading puns and to call the whole thing off.

And there was the pet rock thing. One day one of us read something on the air we had seen on the news wire about someone in California talking about his pet rock. Right away, as a gag, someone sent us a rock and asked us to take care of it while he was on vacation in Florida. That started an avalanche. People just kept sending us pet rocks of all kinds. There were lumpy envelopes all over the station.

Our association with Children's Hospital began in a very offhand way. We never set about to be fund raisers for the hospital. It all began when we spoke to an organization and afterward they offered to donate an honorarium to our favorite charity. We didn't have a favorite charity, but just off the top of his head, Jackson blurted out, "Children's Hospital."

The next day we mentioned this on the air, and suddenly people began sending us checks for Children's Hospital. We would thank the sender for the check, then the number of checks began to multiply. Never once did we *ask* for a contribution, people just sent them. And donations began to take different forms. Organizations would send us public service announcements to read on the air and sometimes tack on a check for Children's Hospital. We read the announcement on the air whether there's a check or not. We even tell people that the check is not necessary, since we don't want anyone to think they have to buy an announcement. Any legitimate public service announcement is going to get on the air. But the checks keep coming in, so we've become big heroes at Children's Hospital.

Now the Harden and Weaver Golf Tournament is an annual event that started in 1970 at Montgomery Village, in Gaithersburg, Maryland. The tournament has raised a million and a quarter dollars so far for the hospital. Since the whole purpose of the tournament was to involve a great number of people, in 1979 we added tennis to increase participation even more.

The idea originated with the late Walter Bogley, who was then managing the Montgomery Village golf course. Walter always wanted to hold a competition to find the best golfer in the entire Washington area. We were sitting around a table one day with Walter and Charles Kettler, whose firm had built Montgomery Village, when the idea came up again. Charles's brother, Clarence, was on the board of Children's Hospital, and it was around this time that the Senators' baseball team had left Washington. For years a special Senators' game had been a charity affair to raise funds for Children's Hospital and it was the source of a big chunk of revenue for the hospital. Suddenly the two ideas came together. A golf tournament at the Montgomery Village golf course would determine the best amateur golfers in the area—and all the proceeds would go to Children's Hospital. To make it widely based, there would be a $5 qualifying fee at each club where the first competitions would be held, and the best golfers at each club would then compete in the finals at the Montgomery Village course. Fortunately as it turned out, the competitive factor became less important, the tournament simply became more like an outing—a fun thing to do. That accounts for its growth. People have a good time and want to take part.

For every golfer who tees off, someone has paid $150. We can handle more than four hundred golfers in our finals. And those who don't play golf can participate in the tennis tournament. Volunteer committees take care of most of the administrative duties along with personnel from Kettler Brothers and from WMAL. The first year we made around $4,000. Last year it grew to well over $100,000—and every penny goes to Children's Hospital. We simply took Walter Bogley's idea and ran with it.

There's no doubt listeners want to participate in activities with us. Back in the late 1960s two or three airlines came to us with the idea of running a vacation trip with us. They said it had been done in other markets, and they thought we could attract a lot of people. But the manager of the station at that time turned thumbs down on the idea. He said he wasn't about to give any free publicity to the airlines. Well, of course, he hadn't listened long enough to find out that the publicity wasn't free for the airlines; they would pay for it. After that manager left, Northwest Orient Airlines came to us again. They said they would buy the time on the air—it would be a commercial transaction—and we'd ask people to accompany us on a trip to . . . wherever. The next thing we needed was a travel agency. So, we thought, why not go with one that had been a sponsor at one time. We searched and the only one we could find was the Bethesda Travel Center, then a little storefront office owned by Tony Adelfio. We went to Tony and asked him if he wanted to promote a vacation tour—that Northwest Orient Airlines wanted to do a tour to the Orient. To say that Tony was overjoyed would be putting it mildly. He had to be restrained from leaping into our arms and smothering us with kisses. We were handling him the key to riches and he knew it.

As luck would have it, we had launched this project, and it was beginning to build, when suddenly Northwest Orient Airlines was hit by a strike, and although Northwest originated the whole idea, they couldn't participate. But another carrier took over. The trip was to Japan, Formosa, the Philippines, Hong Kong and Hawaii. This was no small potatoes. The trip cost about $3,000 per person. And the travel agency couldn't believe the response. When we did this for the first time in 1972, it had been done in other markets—Minneapolis and Pittsburgh—and thirty to thirty-five people made a successful trip. By the time we closed down reservations, 120 people had signed up. Since then we've taken trips to Greece, Italy, Turkey, Africa, Scandinavia, the South Pacific and China. Ninety people went with us to Africa. The China trip was a package that cost up to $3,500, and there was a waiting list. We took eighty people and had to split the group into two sections. The trips are always booked solid. A nucleus of about a dozen people from the first trip have gone on every one of them since. They phone us, or write a letter, wanting to know where we're going next and make sure to include them. The people who have accompanied us range in age from eight to eighty-eight.

Starting with the fifth anniversary of the *Harden and Weaver* show, we've done such programs every five years in a place where listeners could see the show, perhaps drop by on their way to work, join us for a few minutes and go about their business. The fifth anniversary program was done from the Statler Hotel. The tenth originated at the Mayflower

Hotel, and the last two, the fifteenth and twentieth anniversary programs, were broadcast from the Kennedy Center. I found it amazing that people began standing at the Kennedy Center at five o'clock in the morning. To see what? A radio show, with not much action, and this was an audience that covered all age groups and occupations.

On one of those anniversary shows, Willard Scott dropped by to say hello, and he also brought us a present—a belly dancer—who went through her gyrations practically on our table. I thought the show was going to get raided.

Guests are always arriving on these anniversary programs, and very often they are people whose names we don't know. In those cases if we are to chat with them on the air, our producer hands us a little card identifying the person so we can conduct the interview accordingly. Once a gentleman sat down and began a conversation with us on the air, and neither Jackson nor I had any idea whom we were talking with. So Jackson finally scribbled a note reading, "Who the hell is this guy?" and handed it to the producer, Connie Adams. Connie scribbled a note back that read, "He's Lincoln Harner—the guy who has been the newscaster on your show for the past year!" Now that may sound pretty stupid on our part, but we had actually never met Lincoln Harner face to face. We were doing the *Harden and Weaver* program from the transmitter building as usual, but by that time all the newscasts were originating from our facilities on Connecticut Avenue. I knew the guy's voice was familiar but I just couldn't place the face!

I believe the demography of Washington is unique. It is not an industrial town, so there are no work shifts. Everyone essentially rises and retires at about the same time. There are many almost parallel strata of society—transient, but not altogether so, because some people may stay here two or three years. You have the foreign-service people—both American and from other countries—who are in and out all the time.

There are professional and business people on the local scene who are a big part of the market, and then you have the blue-collar workers. I don't know why Harden and Weaver cut across all of this. But at these anniversary affairs—there are people from all those groups. We've gone to many white-tie functions at the ambassadorial or top business level, and the guy who parks the car asks for our autograph, as does the guest of honor at the head table.

One listener moved away from Washington eight years ago and still calls us regularly from Buxton, North Carolina. Others who leave town keep sending us letters to keep us posted on how they're doing. We've had requests from foreign-service personnel from as far away as Australia asking us to send air checks of the program—on tape, commercials and all. We get similar requests from ships at sea.

In Washington you never know who may be listening. Every so often I'm apt to talk about something on the air that I read in the morning paper. One day there was a story about an experimental plane that was being tested—some "X whatever." I mentioned that this plane had gone on a test flight somewhere in California. A few minutes later the phone rang and Jackson picked it up. He said, "Frank, it's for you." I asked, "Who is it?" He said, "A man who says he is Curtis LeMay." I took the phone thinking, "What have I put my foot into now?" The Chief of the Strategic Air Command said something like "Mr. Harden, that experimental aircraft you referred to as the X whatever is really the X so-and-so," and proceeded to tell me more than I could ever comprehend about the plane and its history. Here it was 6:15 in the morning and one of my silly mistakes prompted a call from General Curtis LeMay to straighten me out!

Another comment we made prompted a letter from Admiral Hyman Rickover that grew into an exchange of correspondence for a time.

We also had a correspondence with Supreme Court Justice

William O. Douglas that culminated in his inviting us to join him on a hike along the C & O Canal towpath. This was when he was very much involved in saving the canal from those who wanted to build a road between Washington and Cumberland, Maryland, along the right-of-way. The hike was his way of pointing out the natural beauty of the route, which should not be disturbed. We figured the idea would be for us to walk along with the justice for a time—then let him do the hiking while we went back home. So we walked with the party for about a hundred yards, and when the photographers stopped taking pictures, we peeled off. I think the justice thought we were going all the way.

The only President who said he listened to us was Gerald Ford. We were serving as MCs for the White House correspondents' dinner once and after we did our bit and had started to leave the podium, Ford took my arm and said, "I listen to you fellows—I used to listen in the car every morning when I was Vice-President—driving in from Alexandria—but I don't catch you that much anymore." I guess he had other things on his mind.

Ford also gave us a little plug another time when we were at the White House. The President was entertaining British Prime Minister Harold Wilson and as he introduced us, he said, "These are the two who wake up Washington on the radio here every morning." The Prime Minister replied, "Ah yes, are you two of those crackerjack boys?" We didn't have the slightest idea what he was talking about, but Jackson went along with the gag. "Oh yes," he said, "that's us all right."

Later we found out that crackerjack boys are funnymen or comedians.

When the Carter administration took office we did a series on teaching people to talk southern. I thought that since I was from Savannah, we'd finally be able really to build up some rapport with the White House. The "talk southern" routine made Walter Kronkite's news program, with Roger

Mudd doing the feature, and it also made *People* magazine—but we never heard even a whisper from the White House.

The response we get from the show can also be illustrated by the stamp avalanche.

One morning I mentioned that we had received a letter with a foreign stamp on it. Our engineer, Bob McKissick, hollered through the glass that separates the studio from the control room, "Save it for me—my daughter collects stamps." So we relayed that information to our listeners, too. It was no big deal—just a casual mention. It wasn't long before the stamps began arriving at the station for us to deliver to Bob. We would acknowledge the arrivals, so it became self-perpetuating. Stamps came from everywhere in the world. Jack Anderson's secretary began sending all envelopes with foreign stamps from his daily mail. The postmaster-general sent a collection of the "Man on the Moon" stamps with the signatures of the astronauts. The head of the mail service in England visited Washington once, heard us talking about the stamps, sent us one of the twenty-fifth anniversary stamps of Queen Elizabeth and Prince Philip, and wrote to Bob about his stamp collection. The most touching response came during the Vietnam War when mothers of soldiers killed in action sent whole albums of stamps their sons had collected when they were kids.

Bob McKissick, who was the first Harden and Weaver engineer, retired in 1974 after suffering two heart attacks and undergoing heart surgery. He still visits the show from time to time. He told us his daughter counted the stamps in one box—one that was almost twice the size of a shoebox—and they totaled more than 12,000. Bob estimates that more than half a million rolled in over the years. He would get calls from kids and organizations asking for any duplicates, and he gave away thousands of stamps. He says he has a three-drawer filing cabinet jammed with envelopes that he hasn't gone through yet. And he is still sent some on occasion.

HARDEN AND WEAVER GALLERY

FRANK: Dr. Willoughby, as our expert on human relations, what is your diagnosis of Mr. Steele's [newscaster] unusual behavior?

WILLOUGHBY: I hesitate to use scientific terms, but I'm afraid in the case of Mr. Steele there are no lay terms to describe his syndrome. If you will pardon me, I'll have to resort to clinical jargon.

FRANK: Go right ahead.

WILLOUGHBY: Well, briefly, he's some kind of a nut.

Jackson: Life in the Talking Place

I used to have to sign the station on the air in the days before we were a twenty-four-hour operation, and I confess I used to play around with the announcements that were required by the FCC. I'd get all the necessary information on, but I'd say things like ". . . our studios and transmitter are located at seventy-one fifteen Greentree Road, in the high-rent district of Bethesda, Maryland."

I did many a sign-off for WMAL-TV as well, and I'd also take liberties with those announcements. One of my favorite endings was ". . . WMAL-TV is owned—lock, stock and barrel—by the *Evening Star.*"

One morning Frank dropped his pencil and leaned down to pick it up, and when he sat up he was laughing uncontrollably. We were on the air and naturally I was moved to ask him what he had found so hilarious. He said, "Jackson, I've been working with you all these years and I've just now discovered that your feet don't touch the floor!"

We were still operating the show from the transmitter site, which was in an isolated area of Bethesda. Frank was still picking and pulling the music in those days, and he was in and out of the studio a great deal. I never paid much attention to where he was at any particular time. One day Frank walked out while a record was playing. I was reading a newspaper or something, and I heard the studio door open and close and just assumed it was Frank who sat down beside me. I turned to say something to him and there was a stranger sitting there. This was shortly after the assassination of Senator Robert Kennedy, and this uninvited guest was heading some kind of movement. He kept saying, "You've got to get this message on the air right away or even worse things will be happening." I thought maybe the *Harden and Weaver* program was being hijacked or something. Frank started to walk into the studio at about that time, saw what was going on and went for help. Enough assistance was mustered to usher the man out of the station. He never got on the air with whatever message he was carrying, but the incident forced management to take another look at security out there in Bethesda.

Although we've had our share of guests on the *Harden and Weaver* program, the format doesn't really lend itself very well to interviews. We just don't have the time. Every so often people drop by, and they end up staying for hours. All we can do is work them in between all the other business, but they don't seem to mind. I think they like the relaxed atmosphere. Muhammad Ali stopped by one day for what was supposed to be a brief appearance, and he stayed around until we went off the air . . . reciting his poems and generally sharing in the A.M. mayhem. George Allen was a frequent visitor when he was coach of the Washington Redskins. He was very active in the Jobs for Youth program and would come by to publicize it. I don't think George ever really knew what it was we were doing, but he seemed to have a good time.

Jimmy Dean would always stay all day. Since I had worked with him for many years on television and radio, he always made it a point to drop by when he was in town. He was the master of what he considered double-entendres. Another person who carried on in a rather salty way when he was a visitor was a British earl.

Most people in show business try to avoid a visit to a morning show. They're night people and they like to sleep in the mornings. So they usually arrive kicking and screaming. But after a while they start to have some fun, then you can't get rid of them. Others who stayed for long periods of time were actor Bill Conrad and talk-show host David Frost, who came to promote his interview with former President Nixon.

The most nervous guest we ever had was Paul Harvey. I don't know why the *Harden and Weaver* show should have intimidated Paul, but I don't think he was very comfortable with us. Paul has been a part of the routine of our program for many years. I'm not sure when it was that we started the business of forgetting his last name, but after a while he became aware that we were bringing him on as Paul What's-His-Name. One time on his program he told a very bad joke—a real groaner—and capped it off by saying, "If anyone asks you where you heard that, tell them you got it from Harden and Weaver in Washington." A couple of months later he mentioned our names again. So I got on the phone and called him in Chicago. He said, "I'm getting letters, telegrams and telephone calls from people in your area telling me what you're doing to me with this Paul What's-His-Name business." I said, "You want us to quit?" He said, "Are you kidding? Keep it up!"

After that he always made reference to us on our anniversaries, and he finally came by the studio that one time.

Another Paul Harvey story: Many years ago when we were doing the *Frank and Jackson* show for the ABC network, one program a week would be a remote—it was done from the Blue Mirror on downtown Fourteenth Street. The Blue Mirror was a nightclub that eventually became a strip joint, but in those days it was just a good night spot that featured name jazz artists. One night around two minutes to air time, we were doing a warm-up when a guy walked in and sat down. I said to Frank, "Isn't that Paul Harvey?" He said, "Damned if it isn't!" So we jumped off the bandstand and went over and introduced ourselves. We told him we were about to go on the air on the network. He said, very quickly, "Don't mention my name!" And we didn't.

In the early days when we broadcast from the transmitter, the news person worked from the same studio. Come news time, Frank would get up and take a break, and the news reporter would sit in Frank's chair. I would introduce the news and also do the commercial inside the newscast. The very first newsman on the *Harden and Weaver* show was Len Deibert. Once he was seated next to me and, following the usual procedure for the commercial break, said, "I'll have the weather forecast after this word from Jackson Weaver." Well, it just so happened there was no commercial in the news that day, so I simply turned to Len and said, "Hello." Len went bananas. He was rolling on the floor and he never *did* give the weather forecast. That may have been one of the things that prompted Len to move into management.

Then there was the case of the newsman who wasn't there. The person in question was Ed Meyer, and in those days, unlike now, one man did all the newscasts on the *Harden and Weaver* show. I never even had to look up while introducing the news—I knew who it would be. By then the newsman was using the other studio—separated by a glass window. Our show only went until nine o'clock in those days (the Breakfast Club show followed) so the last newscast was at 8:30. This day I introduced the news, then looked up only to discover that Ed was not there. While I launched into a commercial—reading it very slowly—Frank went off in search of the newsman, figuring he couldn't be too far away. I kept stalling for time, but it became rather obvious that we didn't have a newsman. Frank's search of the building proved fruitless; finally he ran into the news studio and found the newscast that Ed had written, so he sat down and did the news himself. Later Ed called in to fill in the other side of the story.

It seems that each morning, right after the 8:30 news, the news director would call Ed and give him his reporting assignment for the day. His chores were finished after giving the news. He would then go to cover some story. This routine never varied. But on this day—for some still unexplained reason—the news director (who was none other than Len Deibert himself) called *before* the 8:30 newscast. Ed had written the material, placed it in the studio, but before it was time to deliver it, the phone rang—it was Deibert giving Ed his day's assignment. Being a creature of habit, as soon as the phone conversation was over, Ed grabbed his notepad, jumped into his car and headed for a trial in Arlington. He was tooling along some miles from the station when over the car radio he heard me introducing the news. He heard me introducing *him!* And he knew something I didn't know—he wasn't in the studio. That's when I looked up and made the same discovery. He later told me he listened to the little drama in horrified fascination, wondering how it was going to turn out, and his first inclination was to keep driving until he reached the Pacific Ocean, at which time he could pitch himself into the water. He figured we would never let him forget it. He was right.

People are always bringing food to the *Harden and Weaver* show. I'm not sure how it all got started. Groups would have bake sales and bring in samples, or some organization would be pushing a cookbook, or it would be some special anniversary. Anyway, it seems like we do nothing but eat on the show. We've had fully catered meals whipped up by real chefs and served by waiters in tuxedos at six o'clock in the morning. The whole thing is a little bizarre. But the engineers and the news people love it—they're the only staffers on duty that early in the morning. By the time the regular staff people arrive, the food is usually just a memory.

We never know what's going to arrive—ice cream cake, Greek pastries, bagels and lox—food of every possible ethnic origin.

One day two gentlemen from Calvert County, Maryland, arrived with a great big roaster pan covered with foil. After they were ushered into the studio, they sat down and said they had a marvelous treat for us. What was in that pan was a whole possum cooked up with sweet potatoes. They took the lid off, and Frank took one look at those potatoes swimming in grease and immediately excused himself. He said something about some important chore that couldn't wait another minute. So I was left there with those two guys and the possum, and they were urging me to dig right in and taste this mess. On the air. The guys in the control room—the engineers—thought this was all very funny and I could see them practically hanging from the chandeliers. I finally had to do it, so I took a little bite-sized portion from this possum and made the appropriate sounds of gustatory delight. It wasn't bad actually, but it wasn't something you would want to tackle at 7:00 A.M. I told my guests I couldn't eat and read the spot announcements at the same time, but Frank and I would surely polish the whole thing off later on. When they left, Harden sneaked back into the studio. He would have left me to do the rest of the program by myself rather than take a chance on being forced to sample possum and sweet potatoes.

* * *

We've played a lot of tricks on our co-workers over the years, but newsman Jim Clarke really got back at us with a vengeance.

Clarke was doing a newscast one morning and said something that prompted me to make a sound effect of sawing on wood. He started to laugh, and by the time the commercial break came, he was roaring. Clarke finally got through the weather, signed off, and we went on about our business. A short time later he walked back into the room looking like he'd been hit by a truck. He was ashen. We asked him what was wrong and he answered, "Well, it happened. I had an idea it would. I just came back to say so long. The old man heard me break up on the air and he just called up and fired me. It's been nice working with you guys." He really looked crushed and made another attempt to talk but couldn't get the words out. I immediately grabbed the telephone and dialed the boss's number so that I could explain that it was all our fault, but before anyone came on the line, I saw Clarke snicker. We'd been had. It was an Academy Award performance.

One of the services that we supplied in the early days was reuniting dogs and cats with their owners. It started off innocently enough and seemed like a good idea. I guess we just never realized how many people get parted from their animals. We would get on the air and describe this or that missing cat or dog, and give a telephone number and suddenly it began raining cats and dogs. We couldn't keep up with the flow. People's animals didn't just get lost once—they'd wander off time and time again. Our program was literally going to the dogs. We found Sargent Shriver's dog for him a couple of times and managed to reunite Ethel Kennedy with hers, and we found a lot of Republican dogs as well. Finally we had to call a halt to the whole doggone business because it was taking up too much program time. We haven't done dog-and-cat announcements for years, but we still get calls from harried owners. When we point out that we don't do the announcements anymore, they say they heard one only yesterday.

We've been very fortunate in the advertisers who have participated in our program. But as you might expect, every now and then we get a bummer of an account. It seems legitimate enough at first, but it turns out to be a bait-and-switch routine, or maybe a restaurant where the food isn't all that good. Of course, we don't have a personal experience with every account, and if it shows up on our program, we're going to do our best to sell it. So there are times when a listener calls up and says, "Hey, guys, I went to that restaurant you two recommended on the air and it's a real cesspool." They're not very happy with us and with good reason apparently. On the other hand, we get calls from listeners who say, "Hey, you don't want to get involved with these people—I've had bad experiences with them," and give us chapter and verse. The listeners are really doing us a favor by warning us. So we go back to the sales department and tell them to check out the situation. I've seen some spots yanked off the air after incidents like that. We have an electronic friendship with our listeners, who feel they know us and don't want to see us get burned, and we are eternally grateful for their warnings.

I'm just as comfortable on the stage as I am on the air. Frankly, I'm a ham and audiences turn me on. Frank claims I soar to unbelievable heights when there are people around. He's just the opposite. When people come into the studio, he would just as soon they left as early as possible. He's a radio performer, more comfortable in front of a microphone, leaving the listener to be the imaginative one. He prefers to set up something to feed that imagination and let it go from there.

Switching from one medium to another isn't that easy. But when we make personal appearances, people expect us to be funny on cue. What we say on the radio amuses them, and they see no reason why we shouldn't be able to do the same at a live performance. Of course, the hazard is that the things you do on radio may not be transferable.

H. Allen Smith, who wrote so many hilarious books, was asked once to appear at a benefit. He asked what they wanted him to do, and they replied, "Just be funny the way you are in your books. Do your thing." And Smith answered, "Well, why don't I just bring my typewriter and sit down and let people watch me type. That's what I do."

Frank: We Regret We Have but Two Lives to Give . . .

You can always depend on promotion people to come up with wild schemes to get their performers noticed by the public. The wilder the schemes are, the better the promotion people like them—especially since *they* don't have to participate. We've been roped into some dillies.

Once, to promote the opening of a new shopping center, they cooked up a balloon race. Jackson was supposed to ride in one of the balloons, while I would be in the other. A great deal of money was spent advertising this exciting event, and everything was all set for the big race except that no one remembered to tell the boss about it. He found out the night before and hit the ceiling. He didn't want his morning men risking life and limb in some hot-air balloon that might take off and not come down until St. Swithin's Day in Bogotá, Colombia. He said, "No soap." But after all the promotion we had to do something, so we staged the "Great Chicken-Out." We went through all the motions, as though we were actually going to race, but after we climbed into the balloons and everything was all set to begin, we both jumped out and began running lickety-split down the street with abject terror (not so difficult to feign) written on our faces. We became known as the great cowards and the race went on without us.

Unfortunately, the same boss wasn't around when they got us on the elephants. The circus arrived as it does each spring at the train freight yards, and as usual there was to be a parade to the National Guard Armory, where the circus would be held. The circus people always line up some local celebrities to participate in this parade, and our promotion people picked Jackson and me to ride atop the elephants. Jackson was wired up with a two-way radio so he could do a broadcast from the back of his beast during the parade.

The day of the march, the weather was foul—cold and drizzly. I also expect the elephants weren't in the best humor after their long train ride from Florida. In any case, one of the trainers helped me get on the animal's back and I became aware almost immediately that this elephant didn't like me. I can't say I cared for him, either. There was a band around the elephant's neck, but it was just an ornament that didn't give you much of anything to grab on to, so I was not feeling particularly at ease. An elephant doesn't look terribly tall from the ground up, but when you're on its back, you might as well be looking down from the World Trade Center. The parade got under way, and we hadn't gone more than a couple of hundred yards when my elephant definitely came to the conclusion that he did not want me on his back. At best, an elephant has a peculiar gait—it's difficult to blend in with its rhythm unless you happen to be Sabu or Tarzan or somebody. But this elephant was doing strange things—shaking his shoulders and performing all sorts of deviations from his normal gait. It did not help my state of mind to look down and see those huge feet that looked like oil drums. I knew that if I fell under those, I'd become a human wafer. I did what any red-blooded American boy would do under the circumstances. I screamed for help. But there was one problem. The head trainer, Gunter Gable Williams, and his helpers were all German, and they didn't know what I was saying. Obviously, the elephants were German, too, because mine was not answering my supplications and, by that time, he had made Jackson's beast nervous as well.

I shouted every German word I could think of—dumpling, *Gesundheit*, *Liebchen*—even Henry Kissinger—but nothing worked. I knew my only hope was to divorce myself from the animal before he filed first. Finally I was able to lean over and push away from him as I jumped from his back. Somehow I managed to land on my feet and not under his. Gunter, the trainer, ran over to me at that point and congratulated me on putting on such a wonderful act. Jackson, seeing me on terra firma, elected to get off his elephant at the next stop. He was broadcasting, but he simply threw the two-way radio unit to me. The city fire chief happened to be riding past at that moment and gave Jackson and me a ride to the armory. I don't know if the elephant ever forgot the incident, but I never will. There isn't a promotion person in the world who will ever get me on top of a pachyderm again.

Our other brush with promotional disaster was at the rodeo. The rodeo at the Capital Centre in Largo, Maryland, had a benefit performance for Children's Hospital. Jackson and I were chosen to participate. The plan was for us to mount a couple of docile horses, which then would walk slowly out to the center of the arena, where the evening's proceeds would be presented to us for Children's Hospital. We would simply take the check and ride off slowly.

Backstage things started badly. Jackson was a little short for this business, and he had trouble getting on his horse. So a rodeo hand formed his hands into a stirrup and boosted him up. But the boost was a little too vigorous. Jackson went right over the top and just managed to keep from hitting the ground by grabbing the saddle horn. But he was hanging there upside down, and the helper had to run around the other side and boost him back onto the horse's back.

Now it was time to head out of the gate and proceed to the center of the arena to receive the check. At the gate was a rodeo hand who was not informed about what was really going on, and as we passed by he noticed the horses were not going very fast, so he slapped each one on the rear. That did it. Both horses took off at full tilt. My horse was in the lead and I looked around and saw stark terror on Jackson's face as the horses continued to gallop instead of walk. It wasn't long before we were in the center of the arena where the man waited with the check, but the horses went right by him—heading for the other side, or maybe clear out of the arena and down the Washington Beltway, for all I knew. I was afraid the horses would decide to come to a sudden stop and catapult Jackson into row 38. Luckily my horse finally responded to the reins and stopped, and when he did Jackson's horse did also. I figured now both horses would walk back to the middle of the arena, but Jackson's took off at a gallop again, he holding on for dear life. The crowd was roaring—they thought Jackson was putting on a great act. Finally the guy in the middle, with help from some hands, was able to grab both horses. He made his little speech, handed us the check and some of the rodeo people walked us off.

Then there was the time the promotion department told us about an idea they had involving some ostriches at the zoo. We just walked away.

HARDEN AND WEAVER GALLERY

DR. HEADCOLD (describing the commencement concert by the college band the previous evening):

. . . and then after the final, rousing strains of the 1812 Overture, the Dean lit up a big fireworks display that spelled out: "Good Luck, Class of '72." I tell you I ain't seen anything so thrilling since I heard Pat Boone sing "God Bless America" at a Tupperware party.

Frank: Apropos of Nothing Much

I guess Jackson and I have been in every grease pit, Chinese kitchen or bowling alley in the area. Every time we get a new client they insist we visit their establishment firsthand—purportedly so that we can talk about it on the air more authoritatively. Sometimes the sales force simply gets overzealous. A sponsor casually mentions he'd like to meet Harden and Weaver sometime. The salesman comes back and tells us that it's absolutely necessary that we go there to appease the client. So we go, and get the feeling right away that the sponsor's wondering what the hell we're doing there.

Once we had a new sponsor from Orange County, Virginia. We didn't know anything about the company, but apparently they knew something about us. It was one of those real estate deals—there was a tract of land that they were dividing up for a vacation complex. You know, "This is where the lake is going to be, and this is where the golf course is going to be . . ." Most of it is in the "going-to-be" stage.

Anyway, the clients said they'd love to show Harden and Weaver the place. Well, this was way down in Louisa, Virginia—about a three-hour trip by car one way—it's not really my idea of a day at the office. But they kept insisting that we had to see the place—that it would be so much easier for us to talk about it on the air with enthusiasm if we saw it first. Furthermore, they said they would send their corporate plane to take us there and back, so it wouldn't be any problem. The plan was we would all have lunch, view the property, then get back in the plane for the forty-five-minute ride back to Washington.

We had never actually seen any of these people. All our conversations had been on the telephone. We were instructed to go to the general aviation terminal at National Airport, where we would be met by the pilot and by Mr. Prentice, a company representative, who would be our host. We got off the show that morning, headed for the airport and, sure enough, we were approached by a man who said, "You must be Harden and Weaver—I'm Fred Prentice, and, of course, you know Mr. Baxter here." We, of course, didn't recognize Mr. Baxter as anyone we had met before, but we offered the usual "Oh sure—how have you been? Nice to see you again" and all that balderdash. And we were off in the little airplane—finally setting down in a pasture in Orange County. We proceeded to a hotel, where we had lunch, and then we spent a couple of hours touring the property—including taking a motorboat trip around the lake so we could see it from every possible angle. Finally we got back to the sales headquarters, and Mr. Baxter announced that he had to go to the restroom. While he was gone, our host asked us, "Who is Mr. Baxter anyway?" I answered, "We don't know—we thought he was with you!" What had happened was the resourceful fellow apparently had heard us talking on the air about this trip we were going to take. When we did the spot announcement each day, we'd mention that we were going down there—that we'd be flying in the company plane out of National Airport—and that we'd be leaving after the show. He arrived at the airport before us, introduced himself to the client as a friend of Harden and Weaver who would be accompanying us on the trip. So this character spent the whole day with us and neither the client nor we had ever seen him before.

Sometimes I manage to attract attention without hardly even trying. There was the time my wife and I went to see a Russian dance troupe at the Kennedy Center Opera House. That seemed an innocent enough venture. It just so happened that this was the night President Nixon was to make his resignation speech, and the theater had made arrangements to carry the address over the sound system so patrons would not miss the historic event. About five minutes before nine, the Russians got off their toes and the curtain was dropped to bring us the Nixon message.

We were sitting just off the center aisle well toward the front of the theater. I had noticed the TV crew roaming around but didn't pay any attention to it. It didn't even occur to me that they were recording sound. The President's speech was under way and the TV crew had just reached me along the aisle, when Nixon was heard to say, "And I have made mistakes." And I blurted out, "Oh Jesus Christ!" Well, wouldn't you know NBC that night had televised a montage of reactions to the President—and there was Frank Harden doing his number coast to coast. I wasn't identified. I was just one of several people whose reactions were recorded for posterity. Of course, the network used the piece again the next morning so that anyone who missed my starring role in the evening got another crack at it the second time around. There were any number of people who recognized me as the culprit, and the station received several calls from irate citizens who didn't appreciate my irreverent reaction to the President, even though his sun was slowly sinking in the west. One lady called me and screamed, "Why can't you keep your opinions to yourself?" I hollered back, "Dammit, I thought I *was!*"

Very often when we are making appearances at functions outside the station, people question us about things that they maintain we said on the air. And very often the things they are referring to never actually got said on the air. In many cases either they invented something we said, or they heard some remark elsewhere and attributed it to us.

Sometimes we do a routine—and it's not anything original—whereby we give the clean punch line to an absolutely dirty story. Of course, we never tell the story itself—that would be out of the question. And of course, those who know the story have no problem filling in the rest. We've had reports of people driving off the road laughing at the punch line. But you'd be surprised at the number who call us later and chastise us for telling a dirty story on the air.

Once we were making an appearance at the Chevy Chase Women's Club. The lady who was going to introduce us happened to be seated next to me, and she asked, "How should I introduce you?" I replied, "It doesn't really matter—just say, 'Here's Harden and Weaver' because if they don't know who we are it won't make much difference." But she said that wouldn't do because we were her favorites and she wanted to say something nice about us. This routine went on all during lunch and the lady was getting more nervous by the minute, picking at her lunch and tearing her napkin into shreds. Finally it came time for the big introduction. She went up and gripped the lectern until her knuckles turned white, and, with her voice quivering, blurted out, "Ladies, it gives me a great deal of pleasure to introduce you to two gentlemen who I enjoy in bed every morning."

One thing we've learned about this business is that you have to be flexible. Surprises are not supposed to surprise you. We come to work early in the morning not always aware of what may await us on the show. Once when we were still out at the transmitter, we arrived at about 5:30 A.M., walked into the kitchen and found two men dressed in silk suits—the kind that never get wrinkled—with briefcases and all kinds of audiovisuals. And with them was a tall, blond woman dressed up like an Indian princess, with the headgear and everything. I said, "What ho—what's this all about?" Well, we hadn't been aware of it, but a new sponsor was joining the *Harden and Weaver* program that morning, Indian Lakes Estates or something like that, one of those deals where you bought your own campsite. I myself had always thought the enchantment of camping was in roaming around and going to different places, but in Indian Lakes Estates you were locked into your own little spot in the woods. It was another one of those "Here's where the lake's gonna be and here's where the mountain's gonna be" projects.

These guys had decided that to get us enthusiastic so that we could do a better selling job, they would come by and show us pictures of the place and really pump us up. And I guess some public relations course somewhere had told them that you should always bring something unusual along, an attention-getter. So they brought the ersatz Indian princess with the blond hair. She didn't say a word the whole time she was there. But you couldn't miss her. They were really gung-ho about their project, and we assured them we would really lay it on when it came time to do the commercial. We went into the studio, got the program under way and finally their big moment came. It was about 9:20 when I turned the copybook page and there was the spot. And I thought, "These people came all the way out here, so we should really do a job for them." We ignored the copy for a minute and started off by telling our listeners how we had talked with the people this very morning, and had seen pictures of the project, and that it was really something to behold. Then I launched into how experienced campers had gone down there. I wanted to say that many of them had their tents pitched before nightfall. But what came out was: "And many of them had their tits pinched before nightfall."

That brought me to a complete stop. Jackson looked at me as if I had taken leave of my senses. The engineer was laughing so hard he was very close to apoplexy. Jackson said, "The time is nine-twenty," and signaled for a record.

We sat back and waited for the phone to ring, but it never did. No one mentioned it. I thought maybe I had dreamed the whole thing. But a few days later, a letter came from the Federal Communications Commission addressed to Mr. Frank Harden. At the top was the name of Commissioner Robert E. Lee. I tore it open, not without some trepidation, and here is the complete text:

> *Dear Frank:*
>
> *Pet perhaps. Fondle maybe. But pinch? Never!*
>
> *Robert E. Lee*
> *Federal Communications Commission*

It doesn't surprise me that Jackson says he wouldn't be apprehensive about trading ad libs with Bob Hope. Jack's quickness is a thing of beauty. He thrives on spontaneity and he is a great counterpuncher. It's fun feeding him lines just to see what he will come up with. All of them won't be gems, but you're sure going to find a couple of sparklers.

One time, before the manned space shots, the United States was testing rocket propulsion and the escape procedure for a manned capsule. I believe it was a Vanguard rocket being tested, and this was before they began the live broadcasts of the space shots. Anyhow, a bulletin came in on the wire that the Vanguard had blown up on the pad—and that the escape hatch had gone flying off somewhere. The newsroom brought the bulletin to me and I read it on the air. When I finished Jackson said, "I can see it now at the Cape. This guy with horn-rimmed glasses shouting, 'Hey, Werner [Von Braun], can I see you for a moment?'"

The outstanding non sequitur of my career came during a personal appearance at the Washingtonian Country Club. This was in the 1960s, when men were wearing their hair longer and I was trying to keep up with the fashion. A woman came up to me and declared, "Mr. Harden—my son is in Vietnam—why don't you get a haircut?"

I don't know why it is but when it snows in Washington, things go bananas. When the first flake hits the ground, kids call the radio station to find out if school has been canceled; others call us to make announcements on the air canceling every gathering of more than two persons scheduled that day; the German School invokes Plan B (whatever that is); and every city, county and federal government worker wants to know whether he or she can stay in bed. It's Snow Phobia. The symptoms are also apparent in varying degrees during sleet, or even during a heavy rain. WMAL goes into a frenzy of its own to cope with this avalanche of telephone requests—beefing up the newsroom staff and taking on the mode of a crisis center.

The key factor is that while everyone else is getting "liberal leave" or a holiday, it is absolutely necessary that radio station personnel go to work. Sometimes if it begins to snow and the forecast is for copious quantities before morning, some of the staff members will arrive the night before to make sure they will be there in the morning. That was the case back around 1960 when it snowed all day. Jackson and I showed up at the transmitter site at around 7:00 P.M., prepared to stay all night. Many of those who normally went home at around 5:00 or 6:00 decided not to chance the roads and to stay. Absolutely no accommodations were available. There were one or two couches, but most people had to sleep on the floor. During the afternoon as the snow continued to fall, one of the announcers had let it be known on the air that we were marooned, so to speak; new arrivals brought sandwiches, and in keeping with the festive atmosphere, some booze even made its way into our midst. While some people elected to go to sleep, others decided to have a party.

As the night wore on, word came from our sister operation—the TV station on Connecticut Avenue—on how they were coping with the situation. And it became known that in contrast to our primitive survival operation, they had called caterers and purveyors of "rent-a-beds" and were enjoying all the comforts of home. The more some of our people lived it up, the more they got carried away with the injustice of the situation. Finally one of the ladies, whose courage seemed to multiply with each drink, decided to make her distaste known to the general manager. She woke him up with a phone call at about 5:00 A.M. and let him know how she felt about the inequities being visited on the people who worked at the transmitter site as opposed to those being catered to at the television station. The phone call was not a good idea. It didn't take the boss long to deduce that some drinking was going on. By the time morning rolled around, the stories had been magnified to epic proportions—stories of bacchanalian ecstasy, Sodom and Gomorrah under the transmitter towers in Bethesda. There was a big meeting of the upper echelons, and the program director was fired, and the lady who had made the phone call was also given notice, and there was generally a big to-do. Had the phone call not been made, the rather meek events of that evening would have passed unnoticed. Instead, as the years passed by, The Night at the Transmitter grew to the point at which it may someday be included in *Playboy*'s "Ribald Classics."

Of all the movies made in Washington, Harden and Weaver have managed to sneak into only one. The picture was *Scorpio*, starring Burt Lancaster. Actually we weren't in the movie—our voices were. In the opening sequence our voices, on various radios around town, are used to establish that the action was taking place in the morning. There was a montage of radios . . . a car radio, a clock radio in a bedroom . . . all with Harden and Weaver doing whatever it is that we do. That was the extent of our Hollywood career. Unfortunately we never met Burt Lancaster and we never saw the movie.

HARDEN AND WEAVER GALLERY

FRANK: Dr. Willoughby—are you all set with that special center you are setting up for the Dallas players who become totally demoralized by the Redskins?

WILLOUGHBY: Yes, and I have made arrangements with the stadium—we can bury some of the players right there—and save the cost of sending the bodies back to Dallas.

FRANK: You must be expecting the worst.

WILLOUGHBY: Oh yes. The Skins are absolutely savage.

Jackson: The Long and the Short of It

When you come to think about it, we really haven't been in too much hot water, considering how many years we've been on the air. When you're ad-libbing your way through four hours of broadcasting a day, something's bound to come out not quite the way you intended, or even if it did, some people are bound to be upset by it. Some of our offhand remarks might seem funny to some, but not funny at all to others. We always fool around with the Paul Harvey segment that comes in the middle of our show. Once we said something about Paul being to the right of Attila the Hun, and we got all kinds of reaction. One person called up and simply shouted: "Well, he's a better American than you are!"

The unique thing about radio is the accessibility of those who perform on it. People who wouldn't take the trouble to write to a newspaper think nothing of calling up a radio station. Sometimes they call up to complain about something to anyone who answers the phone, and become almost speechless when they find out that the individual they've called to complain about is the person on the line with them. They didn't intend to file their complaint that directly!

The only real trouble we've had, if you want to call it that, involved the Federal Communications Commission.

Everyone knows that one of the things we've done for years is to take certain liberties with the commercials. We'll start into a commercial, then fool around with it, digress for a while and finally get back to it. The FCC had no quarrel with that as such. But when they checked the program log, they noted that the commercials were logged at, say, one minute. Frank has always kept the announcers' log—just as he serves as the coordinator of the program. This relieves me of all those duties so that I can do all the weird bits on the air without worrying about time requirements and all the other workaday procedures. Now—getting back to the commercials—we may launch into a spot that's supposed to be sixty seconds long, but it will actually take us a minute and a half because I ad-libbed in the middle about who knows what. Or we may have used the spot to launch into anything else that came along. Before we've finished the commercial, it's as if we dropped an egg and it's all over the place. Frank would still log the spot as one minute if the log called for one minute. Now, on occasion we may have done the spot in forty-five seconds, but he'd still put down a minute to make it conform to the log.

Well, of course we didn't know it, but after doing this for fifteen years, we were suddenly being monitored. Why or by whom we never knew, but obviously someone put a bug in the FCC's ear. So, suddenly we were cited. A letter was sent to the station accusing us of being in violation of certain rules pertaining to keeping an accurate log. It said the station should show cause why we should not be fined $5,000.

We argued the case by trying to get the FCC staff to tell us what they considered commercial if we went off on a tangent in the middle of the spot, doing material that had nothing to do with the client. We asked if such noncommercial material could be subtracted from the commercial time. They said no. From the first mention of Harry's Used Car Lot to the last mention of Harry's Used Car Lot—it all had to be counted. Sometimes there's supposed to be a tag line on the end of a commercial that we forget about. We play a record, then remember the tag line and do it. The record has to be considered as commercial time. Again, if we logged it as such—they'd have no argument with us. It was all very bureaucratic and silly. But it was a real downer for us because we knew it was the end of a very entertaining aspect of our program.

Frank and I decided to go down and talk the situation over personally with the commissioners—to make them explain this foolishness firsthand. As you probably know, in Washington you have to make an appointment to go to the toilet. But we simply went down there unannounced and walked into each of the commissioners' offices. Secretaries would look up and say, "Harden and Weaver! What are you doing here?" We got to see all but two of the commissioners, and most of them told us how they enjoyed our program, and there was a lot of friendly give-and-take. They told us they realized that what we did was not what the law was designed to protect against. But they said it was something that could lead to abuses. We suggested that instead of citing us, they should write us a letter ordering us not to do it anymore and make the letter public. But they said they couldn't make any exceptions. In a sense maybe they were right. I remember once in New York, a disk jockey was selling a vacation trip to Greece for an airline. He was getting a free trip out of it and would go on the air to do about eight or nine minutes plugging it. That's abuse, no doubt about it.

So the FCC argued the Harden and Weaver case formally for several hours, then cited us and fined us $5,000 . . . even though one commissioner suggested that instead of fining us they give us a medal. The whole incident brought loads of publicity—stories in *The New York Times* and the *Wall Street Journal* as well as in all the trade publications. And would you believe it? People started sending donations to pay

Announcing the arrival of the Harden and Weaver show on the Washington scene, 1960

Frank, 1955, before discovering that profundity didn't pay

Jackson as matinee idol, circa 1955

First TV publicity shots, 1960. (Courtesy Del Ankers Photography)

Harden and Weaver—an afterthought of the Cherry Blossom Festival Parade, 1964. (Courtesy City News Bureau)

Second publicity photograph, 1965

Frank and Jack greeting fans at the International Boat Show in Washington, 1968 (Washington Star Collection—D.C. Public Library)

Frank, in a familiar studio activity, 1976

Jackson, 1976 (Washington Star Collection—D.C. Public Library)

Mrs. Berit Harden

Captain Jack and home away from home

Presenting proceeds from Harden and Weaver Golf and Tennis Tournament to Children's Hospital, 1980. Mrs. Oriana McKinnon (right) *accepts.*

After a five-minute workout at Maryland University's Byrd Stadium, Frank and Jack decide to stick to radio, 1968.

Elsie and Jackson Weaver

Harden and Weaver stand on their record in Washington

our fine. We had to head that off immediately and sent the money back in those cases where we had addresses for the donors. The rest we just sent to Children's Hospital.

But the fine was the least of the problems. Now program people were in the studio with stopwatches timing our commercials as we did them. People kept calling us to tell us exactly how long a commercial ran. No matter what inspiration we may have had during a commercial, we fought back the urge. Commercials became simply commercials. Over the months, however, we began slipping back into our old ways—but of course keeping accurate logs. And now the administration and the FCC have deregulated, and when they refer to that whole area of commercial time and log keeping, they have a new name for it. They call it the Harden and Weaver rule. Such fame for only $5,000!

HARDEN AND WEAVER GALLERY

FRANK: Why are you talking about religion? You don't know anything about religion.

WOMAN: Of course I do. What do you think I am—an amethyst?

Jackson: About This Union, Jack

On occasion British vessels arrive at the U.S. Navy Yard in Washington on courtesy calls.

Once the British Embassy called to say that one of their ships was making a friendship visit and would be open to the public. We usually made announcements to that effect on the air, and this time we were asked if we might help some of the crew members meet some local people, ordinary citizens, not the usual officially arranged stuff. We thought that was a great idea. We set up a routine where people would call up the ship and invite some of the men to dinner, or take them out to the theater, or what have you. The ship personnel then got a special phone number, which the officer of the deck was assigned to answer and to take down all the information when people called with their invitations. We began publicizing this on the air—when the ship would arrive and when people could call that special number. After the ship was in port for a few days, we decided to call that number ourselves to see how they were doing. The officer answering the phone didn't know who we were, and he said, "I hope you're not calling for one of us, sir, we've all been spoken for." There were more than two hundred men aboard the ship, and Washington area people took them everywhere—to their homes, sporting events, sightseeing—everywhere.

There was a little sequel to this story. About four or five months after the ship had left, we got a letter from a woman who wanted to know how she could get in touch with one of the chaps from the ship whom she had entertained. We ignored her letter because we didn't quite know how to answer it. But then she called us and explained that she'd been in touch with the embassy and the naval attaché, but could not learn the location of yeoman so-and-so.

Of course, we couldn't help her either. We don't know if she ever *did* find the father of Little Alfie.

Jackson: "And Then I Said to the Queen . . ."

We get a lot of invitations to appear at various functions just as guests. I expect we receive twenty-five for every one we can accept. But one we jumped at was an invitation from the British Embassy to attend a garden party for Queen Elizabeth when she was in Washington. The invitation came from the British Ambassador, and at the bottom of it were the words "casual dress." We had no idea what the British considered casual dress. I mean, casual dress at the Court of St. James's could mean top hat and tails, for all we knew. So we called the embassy, and they informed us that casual dress meant "whatever one wears to business." I knew they didn't mean what WE wear to business at the studio, because Frank wears short-sleeved T-shirts even in the winter, and my clothes are usually the ones I wear aboard my tugboat. Furthermore, Frank went home and discovered that although he had many sports jackets, he didn't own a suit. So he went out and bought a three-piece suit for the occasion, and to this day his wife refers to it as "the Queen's suit."

On that great occasion of the Queen's visit, there were around sixty of us assembled in the garden at the embassy on Massachusetts Avenue. Presently the Queen's man—or whatever you call him—came out and explained the rules of the game to us. He told us it wasn't necessary to bow or curtsy. But he said we were not, under any circumstances, to touch the Queen or Prince Philip. In other words, no matter how friendly she is, don't slap her on the back after a funny line. He indicated the door through which the Queen and the Prince would be entering the garden, and he said we were casually to form a line and pay our respects one by one. He told us when that was all finished, the Queen would go wherever she wanted—chat with whatever group she chose to approach.

Finally the Queen made her entrance and we all looked at each other kind of petrified—no one wanted to make the first move to form the line.

So I said, "Let's go, Frank—somebody's got to break the ice or this will be a tableau for the next thirty minutes." We walked over to the Queen and introduced ourselves, and that started the ball rolling. Finally the reception line ran out and everybody went off in different groups making conversation and wondering what the Queen would do next. I looked up and saw she was making a beeline straight for us. I said, "Frank, don't look now, but here she comes!" Sure enough, Her Majesty strolled over to us and said, "So you're broadcasters, are you—just what is it that you do?" We explained that people have been trying to figure that out for years, but we told her about our morning show, and I also decided to give a good plug for the British Embassy Players—a theatrical group that performed there. Of course, she didn't know anything about that, and I said, "Your Majesty, even the Ambassador, Lord Ramsbottom, sang a song in the last production." And she said, "My—and all the time I thought he was working." I said, "And he brought the house down, too." The Queen looked a little puzzled. "Brought the house down?" She shook her head and walked away. I think she thought I was going to slap her on the back.

Frank: The Big Apple Beckons

It was sometime in the early seventies that we got a call from the program director of WNBC in New York, asking us if we had ever thought of the possibility of working in Manhattan. We told him that we were very happy in Washington, and besides, we still had a couple of years on our contract at WMAL. He answered that those kinds of problems could be worked out and suggested that at least we come up there and talk about it. We thought that could do no harm, it's always flattering to know that the nation's number one market is interested in little old you. I guess it's somewhat like trying out for a part in a play that you really don't want to be in—it's the challenge of winning the part that counts. So we got on an airplane one morning and headed for New York to see why anyone thought New York was ready for Harden and Weaver. (Did those guys know we play a hymn in the morning?)

We had lunch with the program director in the executive dining room at the RCA Building, and he said he saw no way that we wouldn't take New York by storm. Then he began to minimize his expectations—noting that as much as an 8 or a 9 share of the audience in New York would be sensational. The market was so big and so highly specialized. Many stations can get a piece of the action and make out very well. It came as a shock to us that no station was looking for dominance—that their goals were much lower. In Washington, Harden and Weaver were doing about a 23 share of the audience. There was talk of money—but it was rather vague. Our host never made any firm offer—he simply told us to go home and talk it over with our families and get back to him if we were interested and wanted to talk specifics.

Jackson and I got into a taxicab heading for La Guardia Airport and we were both silent. I looked at him and he looked at me and we both shook our heads and that was the end of our flirtation with New York.

I suppose if this had all come up when we were in our twenties rather than in our forties, we would have figured we had died and gone to heaven. I probably would have stayed right there, checked into the YMCA and said, "I'm ready to start whenever you want me." But we'd done the *Harden and Weaver* show for ten years. We were comfortable with it—much of what we did was based on our knowledge of the Washington area. We loved Washington and the station and didn't want to uproot our families for something that could be as ephemeral as New York radio. WNBC then hired Imus, who became a well-known personality as "Imus in the Morning."

Despite the success of Harden and Weaver, there have been no other direct job offers from anyone. We usually sign a contract in five-year increments and I suppose the industry is aware we do that.

Jackson: Weaver and Weaver

People are always getting Frank and me mixed up. Whenever I get a little confused myself about who I am, I always head for home because Elsie is there and she can tell us apart right away. Elsie and I have been married for thirty-two years. The Bible says a man who has found a good wife has found a fine thing, and I feel I have been blessed in that department. I had been married before—to a high school sweetheart—a marriage that never really got off the ground and ended in divorce.

I met Elsie in 1949 when I was still working out of the Trans-Lux Building in downtown Washington. It was my habit to skip across the street to eat breakfast at Sam Dean's Crescent Café. Working there as a waitress was young Elsie Stiff, who had come up from Thaxton, Virginia, with her sisters, Nellie and Marie, to work in the big city. During the war years, Elsie had worked at the Hercules Powder Company plant in Radford, Virginia, helping to turn out ammunition for the war effort. She actually became aware of Jackson Weaver at that time, because she always listened to the program *Victory Parade of Spotlight Bands* and had become familiar with the announcers' voices. Anyhow, it didn't take too many scrambled eggs at Sam Dean's before I was in love with Elsie, and there came a time not too long thereafter when the feeling became mutual. There was one problem.

Elsie already had a boyfriend and he wasn't going to give up without a fight. And I mean a *real* fight!

I was driving down Fourteenth Street one summer afternoon accompanied by Elsie and her two sisters, when I was suddenly forced to the curb by another car. Elsie immediately informed me that the two angry people in the other car were her boyfriend and his uncle. The two men and I bailed out of our cars, and the battle was on. Very soon a crowd of about fifty people had formed a circle around us there in the middle of the street. At that instant, what I could have used most was a cop. But as they say, "When you need a cop, etc." This was a black neighborhood, and most of the people seemed to be cheering for me—the little guy with the big moustache. However, I suspect all bets were being placed the other way. We'd been going at it for a while when I heard a woman say to her companion, "You get in there and help that little man before he gets himself killed!" That was very cheering news because things had not been going my way. I had taken a crashing blow from Uncle that sent me to the pavement, but not before I had banged my head against the chrome bumper of a parked car. However, my new benefactor turned the tide and chased off the bully boys, and the fight was over. I managed to drive to the old Ear, Eye, Nose and Throat Hospital near Thomas Circle, where they stopped the flow of blood from my ear, eye, nose and throat as well as from several newly created orifices.

It took a little longer to permanently discourage the boyfriend, but eventually Elsie and I began a less hectic romance. I even drove my big Lincoln four-door sedan into the heart of the Confederacy to meet Elsie's mother in Thaxton, and I was not set upon as being either a carpetbagger or a "revenoor." That was a good thing because I don't think my insurance covered that.

Elsie and I were married in 1950, and she is a patient,

long-suffering wife who has had to put up with my shenanigans and weird hours on the job. We have three sons. Mark is a newscaster with Associated Press radio, and lives in Gaithersburg, Maryland. Scotty is the outdoor type—he lives in Denver, where he repairs big diesel equipment, and is married. Our third son, Eric, is also married and is in the printing trade. He has provided us with our grandchildren, Natalie and Leah.

Frank: Light the Trip Fantastic

We've managed to escort any number of people to various parts of the world without getting into too much trouble. Naturally the law of averages catches up with you once in a while.

Even though we are, in a way, the leaders of the expeditions, we are not travel agents and we are not tour guides. And the thing we definitely are not is the complaint department. In other words, if the sink in your hotel bathroom doesn't work, don't come to us.

We were traveling in Scandinavia one time with a group of about sixty-five persons, including a lady who lived in the Washington area and her mother. The mother, I would guess, was in her late sixties. We were in a lodging in a little village one morning having breakfast, when the daughter came over to my table to inform me that her mother wasn't feeling well. My first thought was "Why is she telling *me* this—what am I expected to do about it?" But I went over to their table to see what assistance I could lend, and just as I got there, the mother toppled right off the chair and onto the floor. I checked her out and, even with my limited knowledge, I could sense no pulse. I picked her up and carried her over to a couch. Fortunately, there was a doctor among those taking the tour, and she arrived on the scene and administered to her until a local physician could get there. The local doctor had to come by boat—but he was there in very short order, diagnosed the lady's problem as some kind of heart seizure and said she would have to be hospitalized. The trip to the hospital was by boat, which was actually the ambulance.

All this presented somewhat of a problem, not only for the mother but for the tour because we were scheduled to leave that day. Our travel agent, Tony Adelfio, made arrangements for the daughter to stay with her mother while the rest of us continued on the next leg of the trip. The idea was we would keep in contact with the daughter and figure out what to do next when the mother's situation clarified. That's exactly what we did. As we went along we spoke from time to time on the telephone with the daughter and, on a couple of occasions, with the mother as well. We assumed that the mother was recovering satisfactorily.

About ten days went by. We were in Copenhagen, and I was having a cocktail party for the group in my suite before we went out to dinner. We just happened to have the little get-together in my suite because it was bigger. I was getting ready for the arrival of the guests when I got a call from Tony Adelfio. He said, "Frank, I think we've got a problem." I asked, "What's up?" And he told me that the ailing woman whom we had left behind had died. He wanted to know how we were going to handle this with the other tour members. I said, "Tony, I don't know any more about that than you do, but I don't think I'd make any big announcement about it. If someone asks, we tell them. Otherwise, we don't say anything." Having solved that in my cowardly way, Tony then told me the woman's daughter would be arriving shortly from Norway and would need a place to stay that night. Hotel rooms were hard to come by—but my room would be vacant that night because my stepdaughter and I were taking a train for Stockholm to meet my wife. I told Tony it would be perfectly O.K. for the daughter to take over my room.

The woman showed up at around five o'clock—about an hour before the party was scheduled to begin. She appeared to be in pretty good spirits after the ordeal she'd just gone through. The first people to appear for the party were Jackson and his wife, Elsie. Now, I never had a chance to inform the Weavers that the lady's mother had died, so of course the first thing Jackson asked her was, "How is your mother?" She said, "My mother died." That took Jackson aback, and he stammered his condolences and finally asked, "Well, where *is* your mother?" She pointed to her suitcase, which was quite visible there in my closet. What she had done was quite logical. She had had her mother's body cremated—and was carrying the ashes back home in her suitcase. By that time the other guests were arriving and I had to take care of them. Later that evening, as I was dressing for dinner, I had to get things out of the closet from time to time. Not once could I do it without thinking about the lady in the suitcase.

Our African trip had us flying out of Nairobi to Cairo with stops, for some reason, at Entebbe in Uganda and at Khartoum in the Sudan. And we flew Aeroflot.

Let me tell you about the "people's airline." I learned a long time ago to take my time on trips like this one—not to rush for the first space on the plane. I found out that if they run out of economy class, they put you in first class at no extra charge. And that's exactly what happened on this trip. Now, if you thought that on the "people's airline," there wouldn't be such a creation of the bourgeoisie as first class, you would be very wrong. This was first class out of *Dr. Zhivago*. It was plush. Jackson was back in economy class with his box lunch while we were served an excellent dinner.

The night before we left Kenya, we had dinner at the Hotel Nairobi and Tony Adelfio thought it would be a good idea to invite the two officers who operated the Aeroflot office there. If you had sent out to Central Casting for two typical Russian officers—these were the guys. They arrived in full uniform, looking very sober and official. One of the first things they wanted to know after we were introduced was if we worked for the Voice of America. We were happy to inform them that we didn't work for the government—that we were in commercial radio. They acted as though they had no idea what commercial radio could be, but it was obvious they would have found it very hard to get very chummy with anybody who worked for the Voice of America. We sat down and had dinner, and the more they ate and drank the more they loosened up, until by the time they left you would have thought we were all fraternity brothers. Then a funny thing happened. The next day at the airport, we had friendly greetings for our new friends—and they acted like they'd never seen us before. Everything was very official again. There was one crack in the deep freeze, though—they gave roses to all the ladies on the Harden and Weaver tour.

The stop in Entebbe was a little strange. Idi Amin was still the man in charge in those days. It was a very beautiful airport and several other planes had arrived, so it was quite busy in the terminal. It featured a number of boutiques—though there wasn't much in them except a picture of Amin. The airline people told us we would be there for about an hour or so, and they gave each of us a chit that was good for one drink at the bar in the terminal.

I wandered over. The bar was rather crowded and there was only one bartender. I decided I would order something simple, just in case I had trouble getting him to understand me. I happened to see a bottle of Campari sitting there, so I pointed to it when he came to take my order. He asked me what I would like with it, and I said soda would be fine. I was just happy to get a drink after waiting forty-five minutes. So, he fixed me a Campari and soda . . . strawberry soda.

Then there was our visit to the radio station in Accra, Ghana. Someone at the United States Information Service contacted us after we arrived, asking us if we would like to be interviewed on Ghana radio. We weren't all that enthusiastic about it, since it was hard to see what kind of interest in us there would be in Ghana—but we went along with the idea. The USIS man arranged for us to visit a disk jockey who was doing a morning show, an English language broadcast, and since we are morning men, he figured we'd have a lot in common.

We drove to the radio station, and we were stopped at the guardhouse by a soldier who was equipped with a rifle, hand grenades and I don't know what else, but he was not your typical radio station receptionist. The USIS man explained why we were there. There was a lot of conversation—all of it leading nowhere. Apparently we weren't on the guard's list of welcome visitors for that day, and he wasn't about to let us past that checkpoint. We told the USIS man that we had no pressing need to go any farther—and if we weren't on the list of the gentleman toting the rifle and hand grenades, we'd just as soon head back to the hotel. So we did.

The next morning, USIS called and told us it was all a big misunderstanding, that today we were sure to be cleared—so we drove over again and he was right. Hand Grenade Harry waved us right through the checkpoint as if we were the inspectors general of the Ghanaian army. The whole radio station complex was like an armed camp. I guess that's not unusual, since usually the ones who control the radio station also control the country—the station is one of the first targets of any coup.

We were ushered into a studio where the morning man was doing his disk jockey show, giving the weather and doing the usual morning show kind of routine. When he interviewed us, it was obvious that he had done his homework. Apparently when he heard we were coming, he was able to get hold of some *Harden and Weaver* broadcasts. It so happened that on one of the "Today in History" routines we did on that particular broadcast, we had commented on the birthday of the onetime heavyweight boxing champion, Joe Louis. One of us had made the offhand remark that Louis was the last great champion we had. Our host jumped all over us—wanting to know why we were ignoring Muhammad Ali. Actually the remark had been made without much thought—we hadn't intended to slight Ali, we just had made one of our meaningless comments. But our interviewer saw something sinister in the fact that we had, by omission, slighted Ali, who was extremely popular in the Third World. The rest of the interview was less controversial and probably less interesting.

As we were leaving the compound, several buses arrived and scores of people got off. The compound consisted of five or six radio stations, and we wondered why some four hundred to five hundred people were arriving. Our Ghanaian guide told us that they were all employed at the radio stations, and he indicated that many of them didn't have much to do but shuffle papers.

Both Jackson and I are honorary members of the Kiwanis club. I suppose we gave speeches at the meetings so often, they just decided to make us members. Kiwanians have a tradition of taking little flags when they visit other countries and present the native Kiwanians with this token of friendship on behalf of their particular chapter.

When it came to the attention of the Georgetown Kiwanis club that Harden and Weaver were going to visit Auckland, New Zealand, we were given the little flag and asked to present it to the club Down Under. Apparently there was also some correspondence with the club in New Zealand as well.

Our trip to Auckland took about twenty hours or so, and after arriving at the airport, we took a bus to the hotel. We were both looking for a chance to refresh ourselves and take it easy—deal with the jet lag and all—before setting out on the town. But as we arrived at the hotel, we were greeted by two men who said they were Kiwanians and were expecting us. They also informed us that we were to be honored guests at a meeting of their club, and there was no time to lose because the meeting was about to get under way. Before we knew it, we were in a car and being transported to this Kiwanis gathering. Do you know what? Kiwanis club meetings are no different in Auckland, New Zealand, than they are in Georgetown. How we ever traveled twenty hours half way around the world and arrived on time at a Kiwanis meeting is beyond my comprehension. We had never arrived on time at the meetings we attended in Georgetown. And after all that, we forgot to give them the flag.

Jackson: We Must Be in China Because I Can't Find H Street

It was a kind of strange feeling flying into Peking. My first impression when we arrived at the airport was "How did the pilot find it?" It was about ten o'clock at night and I never saw the runway. Then in the terminal there were no other people. It was a huge airport but except for a couple of sixty-watt bulbs, there were no lights and no activity. We got our luggage and boarded buses to our hotel in downtown Peking, and the trip was a little weird. Every few blocks there would be a dim streetlight—and a large congregation of people under each of those lights. Everything was going on—men playing cards, kids jumping around, and it was like that all the way into the center of Peking.

In the city apparently there are three classes of hotels. One class is strictly for tourists. Another is for Chinese who live elsewhere and are visiting for some reason. The third is for the local people. All of the hotels look like they had been built in the 1930s and the crew that built them had walked away and had never done anything to them again. There was nothing wrong with the hotels. They were decent, clean accommodations. But they looked as if they had been used in at least seven Humphrey Bogart movies; they fairly reeked with intrigue. The hotels apparently have no problems with theft—people just left their doors open. A young man was on duty at a desk on each floor—you left the key with him if you locked up. When you got back you didn't have to tell him the room number, he had it down pat. Apparently we don't all look the same! He also took care of your laundry.

Besides Peking, we visited Shanghai, Hangchow and Canton—and we seemed to have complete freedom of movement. Of course, we weren't looking for any top-secret activities . . . and weren't going off on any field trips in search of the Boxer Rebellion.

We made trips to several communes, and the visits apparently all went according to the same script, whether it was a tea commune, a farm commune or an industrial commune. What happened was, you walked in and they took you to a central hall. It had a big conference table with chairs around it. On the walls were pictures of Marx, Lenin, Stalin and Mao. You sat down, and the guide, who spoke English, introduced you to the head guy of the commune. This person was elected to the job. The head guy probably could speak English, too—but he didn't. He gave his little talk in Chinese, explaining all about how the commune worked, and the guide interpreted it for you. Then the meeting was thrown open to questions. You were told to ask anything you wanted to. Then you made your abbreviated tour around the place.

One of the communes appeared to be more prosperous than the others. It was a tea commune, and the manager seemed very proud of all the features it boasted. It had a higher education program and early retirement for older workers and other goodies. The manager was pretty frank about it—he said this was by no means a typical commune.

We also got to visit various homes in a commune and were allowed to chat with the people living there. At one house we found a man who said his wife was a schoolteacher. We asked him about his children, and he told us his daughter was on a collective farm. I asked, "Does she like it there?" He answered, "No. She was told to go there." I asked him if she would ever be allowed back, and he said the only chance would be if he or his wife retired and the daughter could qualify for either of their jobs—or if she met a boy and they got permission to look for jobs at the commune. He wasn't at all reluctant to discuss how lives were controlled by the state.

In the cities the shops were well stocked with goods and crowded with people. The service was immediate—no waiting around for clerks to wait on you.

When you go to China they exchange your money for "funny money," or scrip. This is to prevent tourists from taking money out of the country. The only trouble with that is some merchants don't know what the funny money is . . . and insist on real Chinese currency.

I was in one store with Elsie, and she spotted some bowls she wanted. When it came time to pay, the guy behind the counter wasn't impressed with our currency. There was a lot of jabbering back and forth, and finally an old lady appeared on the scene, gave a quick course in Monetary Science 301 and the guy finally caved in. I wonder what would have happened if I had given him my Visa card. I'd probably be on a collective farm.

Jackson: "What Does That Ostrich See in Me, Anyway?"

Of all our trips, the one to Africa offered the most of everything. Right near the Tsavo National Park is the Kenya Safari Club, which has to be one of the most luxurious places in the world . . . with its sunken marble bathtubs, its manicured grounds and its prices. The sun sparkling on Mt. Kenya is a sight that almost takes your breath away.

One day we piled into our Volkswagen mini-buses and went on our version of a safari. There were thirteen buses, and at one point we rounded a bend and came to a screeching halt because there were two rhinos in the middle of the road. Since rhinos weigh four and a half tons each they have the right-of-way. We stopped and watched them for a while, and apparently one of them said to the other, "What do you say we scare them a little bit?" Then they laid their ears back and started to paw the ground. It was at that point that our guide suggested we leave. He said when rhinos get their minds made up, they'll even charge a locomotive. I'm not sure how much they charge a locomotive. And their eyesight is worse than Frank's—they're not sure who they're wiping out and they don't care. They know where you are because they smell well. Actually they smell bad, but they have a good sense of smell.

While on safari we ran across hundreds of baboons. When we stopped to take some pictures of them, one of the critters reached into the bus, grabbed a lady's overnight case and took off. He scattered underwear all over the place as he went.

But the most unsettling thing of all was the way the ostriches ran alongside your car, looking in the window. Here you're going around twenty miles an hour, and this ostrich is keeping right up with you—with no trouble at all—and he's staring at you through the window! You get to thinking, "What's he trying to prove—what does he really want?" It's a real trip.

On our way to Greece on one of our trips we stopped at the airport in Rome. We happened to arrive not long after a terrorist shoot-out at the Athens Airport, so security at the Rome airport was tighter than usual. Customs went through our bags about a dozen times. Since I'm a diabetic, I have to carry insulin and syringes with me wherever I go, and when they found this material in my luggage, it almost touched off an international incident. There was a big conference while I kept saying, "Medicine, medicine!" Finally somebody who could understand English came by and was able to explain that I wasn't some kind of drug pusher.

I suppose this happens to most everybody, but it seems that no matter where we go, we run into people from the Washington area. One day we were in the Imperial Hotel in Tokyo waiting for an elevator when we heard someone call out our names. It was a businessman from Washington who was there trying to sell the Japanese some kind of airplane.

Once we were walking down the street in Paris, and a lady came up to Frank and said, "It can't be!" She was the assistant principal at the grade school where Frank's daughter was a student.

In Mombasa, on the Indian Ocean, we were having lunch when a couple spotted us. They had lived for a time in Washington and now were with the NASA tracking station.

Frank: On the Road

From time to time our program originates from other places. There is no particular reason for this except maybe to provide a change of pace, and our listeners seem to enjoy it vicariously. The program remains pretty much the same no matter where we are, although we probably have more guests when the show is on location. Our most ambitious remote broadcast was a three-day affair from London a few years ago. Friends at the British Embassy came up with the idea, and we could find no compelling reasons why we shouldn't do it. Convincing us was easy, but we had to sell it to management. It's not like doing the program from a shopping mall. But an account executive, Carol Highsmith, worked on getting some English sponsors, including British Airways, Burberry and Rolls-Royce, and we were in business.

Before we left, the station took a huge ad in *The New York Times,* calling attention to the trip since it was a first for a local station to be doing this. And ABC had a big party for Harden and Weaver at Studio 54 in New York as sort of a bon-voyage gala. Actually it was held for the national reps and the ad agencies. The next day Harden and Weaver, our wives, producer Connie Adams and Chief Engineer J. B. McPherson all flew to London in a Concorde and set up shop at the BBC's Radio London studios.

The BBC's cooperation was unstinting—anything we needed for the broadcast was made available. I got the feeling that they would have torn down some walls if that would make us more comfortable. The show was on the air from noon until 4:00 P.M. London time. We had no trouble lining up guests, including Ingrid Bergman, who was appearing in a play in London at the time. We also interviewed the Lord Mayor of London, and the Governor and Chief Beefeater of the Tower of London. The latter two had visited the *Harden and Weaver* show when they were in Washington a while ago and at the time, they had said we should look them up if we ever got to London. We did, and they were gracious guests. We also talked on the air with Sykes and Edwards, two famous British comedians, and with the King and Queen of the Pearlies. The Pearlies are street players who appear at benefits and other functions. They are recognizable by their clothing—every inch of which is covered with buttons—hence the name Pearlies.

The transatlantic broadcasts went rather smoothly, and after three days we packed up and headed back to Washington.

Another of our remotes took us to Montreal. We went there at the invitation of John Bunt of the Canadian Tourist Bureau who was a big fan of the show. The first idea was that Harden and Weaver would take a tour of Canada, strictly on our own, but we thought it would be a good place from which to originate a broadcast. It wasn't long before we got an invitation, with the CBC supplying the studio space and the necessary engineering. They also assigned us a producer, and we did the show from the Hotel Bonaventure on a Friday and Saturday in October. Our host was a gentleman named Benoit Balanguer, who was the assistant to the mayor of Montreal. On the air we spent a good bit of time extolling the virtues of the city, which indeed has much to offer, and I guess everyone was happy because we've been invited back.

We've taken the show to Key West, Florida, twice. Our

purpose was strictly to head for some place that was warm in winter. I'd been to Key West before, and I thought it would be an interesting originating point. It all came together when Marriott built a new resort hotel there. Since Marriott is one of the station's accounts, it was logical that we would do the show from Key West. A reporter for the *Miami Herald* interviewed us, and one of the questions he asked was "Why are you doing your show here?" My answer was "Why not?" He accepted that, and the headline on the story he wrote read, "They Said They Wanted Some Time in the Sun and They Got It."

At least twenty couples—all Harden and Weaver listeners—came down from the Washington area. Others, former listeners who had moved to Florida, also appeared. We did the show outside on the patio as people gathered for breakfast, and there was a good crowd on hand to hear Harden and Weaver read one commercial after another—just like back home. But it sure beat being in Washington in January.

Another traditional spot now is Rehoboth Beach. Since Rehoboth bills itself as the nation's summer capital, it's a logical place in which to do a broadcast to herald the opening of the season each Memorial Day. We simply see ourselves as the vanguard of the big trek to the beach each summer. Our broadcasts are from Slicker's Restaurant at the Henlopen Hotel, which is usually filled for around three breakfast sittings during the four hours we're on the air. It's a very festive atmosphere.

HARDEN AND WEAVER GALLERY

STOKES: Which one of you is Jackson Weaver—the tall, skinny one?

WEAVER: No—me—the short, fat one.

STOKES: Mr. Weaver, I can't find you on the company payroll.

WEAVER: Well, that's understandable—I've only worked here for twenty-eight years.

STOKES: I've looked under Accounts Receivable, General Salaries, Debits, Credits, Accounts Payable, and I can't find your salary listed anywhere.

WEAVER: Have you tried Petty Cash?

Frank: Life Begins at 3:45

If there is one aspect of our job that makes people recoil in horror, it is the fact that we have to get up so early in the morning.

Once you tell someone that you actually rise at 3:45 A.M., they want to know how you manage to cope with something so unnatural. They want to know what time you go to bed, how your family can deal with this obvious disruption, and they are certain that it forces a Spartan existence upon you.

The fact is, you just have to set your priorities. If work is the most important thing, then you backtime to arrange everything else around it. I don't feel that I deprive myself because of those hours. I go to the theater when there's something I want to see—although at $30 a pop, I find less and less that I want to see. There were times in my career when I partied until it was time to go to work. But at our age, we no longer have the kind of life-style that might present a problem. I try to get to bed each evening by ten or eleven o'clock. I don't even own an alarm clock. No matter what time I go to bed, I wake up automatically at 3:45 A.M. Jackson uses an alarm clock. I don't think he's ever been late to work. And every morning he stops off at Ernie Caudill's Bethesda Community Store, buys two big cups of coffee and brings them to work with him. He gives one of them away. We have all the coffee anybody could possibly drink at the station . . . but Jackson stops at that store because that was his routine when we did the show from the transmitter and Jackson is a creature of habit. He also remembers that on holidays when the store was closed, Ernie or Margaret Caudill would take a pot of coffee out to the transmitter to make sure that the troops would have some java. Also—Ernie's coffee is better!

Back in 1966 the Washington area was hit by a blizzard that left nearly two feet of snow before it ended in the evening. During the afternoon as the snow was falling, Jackson made arrangements with the WMAL police helicopter to pick him up and take him to work. He lived across the street from an elementary school where there was a large parking lot and no overhead wires. He was to go out there at four o'clock in the morning and stand in the middle of the parking lot, waving a flashlight. He had to wade through snow up to his waist, but he got there and waved his flashlight, and sure enough, the chopper came on cue and picked him up and took him to work. Usually on snow days we have the easiest time of all because there's no traffic to hinder us—we have the roads all to ourselves.

We've said it many times—we feel we are like a utility. When people flip on the radio in the morning, they expect us to be there. I guess that's why I am very impatient with those who use the slightest excuse to avoid doing something. With a complete lack of tolerance, I always say that anyone who would stay home from work because of a headache or a hangover or even a nagging arthritic pain, as they say in the TV commercials, really didn't want to go to work in the first place. There are many people who interpret their employer's sick-leave policy to mean that many more days of vacation. Whether they are ill or not, it's "Use up that sick leave—you've got it coming."

I guess I shouldn't take any credit for an accomplishment that comes naturally or instinctively, but the fact is that in thirty-five years with the same company, my total sick leave amounts to less than thirty days. I don't mean thirty days a year—I mean thirty days in all. Jackson's record is even better than that.

During my thirty-five years with the company, I had a couple of brushes with the Grim Reaper.

The first episode occurred in 1954, when I awoke one morning to discover that I had no equilibrium. I couldn't even get out of bed. As a matter of fact, I couldn't even raise up on one elbow without falling back down.

"Something is definitely amiss," I confided to myself.

Mrs. Harden struggled to get me dressed and down to the medical complex at Eighteenth and I streets, N.W., where Dr. Arthur Morris administered an electroencephalogram and other tests and discovered that indeed something was amiss. There was an aneurysm ballooning in my brain and about to erupt—a condition that called for immediate remedy: ligation of a carotid artery. That means, I believe, that one blood supply to the brain was cut off at the pass to relieve the pressure on the offending vessel, thereby also relieving the unwanted pressure on the part of the brain that controls equilibrium. I sport a silver clip in my neck to this day. (And to this day, that little clip is always noted as "unidentified foreign matter" on my periodic chest X-rays). Anyway ten days later, with my balance and stability restored, I was back at the factory.

Then on Easter Sunday, April 15, 1963—when the *Harden and Weaver* show was three years old—I had a real scary episode. I mean, catastrophe falls far short of characterizing it.

I was at home alone, acting depressed about all kinds of

things—income tax time, aberrations in my domestic tranquillity—and just not feeling well in general. As a matter of fact, I was in bed . . . alternately reading and thinking dark, unpleasant thoughts, when suddenly I realized I was completely without strength and was becoming nauseated. My concern about how I was going to make it to the bathroom a few steps away ended when I stood up and regurgitated what appeared to be at least ten gallons of blood. It probably amounted to a couple of teacups full, but on that white carpet and in those surroundings, it looked like every liter in my body. It developed that my esophagus had become unglued. I was too weak to get up from the floor where I had fallen, and there was no one in the house to call. I can remember the thoughts that crossed my mind at that instant. They weren't too original. I said to myself, "Well, I'm gonna die right here and now." Then I wondered how the hell I was going to get that mess cleaned up before that BIG EVENT happened. *After* it happened would be too late. Then an old Laurel and Hardy line came to me: "A fine mess . . ."

The next step was pretty dramatic even for a slow-moving TV drama. I pulled the telephone down from the nightstand. It clattered to the floor, and I mustered enough strength to dial "O," and with the receiver on the floor and my head next to it, I tried to explain to the operator what kind of a predicament she was to get me out of. Let me say that I can't go along with the old clichés and caricatures about dumb, nonunderstanding, stereotyped telephone operators. Because this operator carefully extracted from me my address, the names and some phone numbers of my neighbors, and all the while tried to comfort me with "It won't be long." (It did occur to me to question her, "It won't be long until what?") Then, within minutes, the Bethesda-Chevy Chase Rescue

Squad arrived, and with sirens screaming, I was on my way to Suburban Hospital.

I never lost consciousness and was able to tell the people in the emergency room the names of doctors and other pertinent information.

There followed an emergency exploratory operation by my friend, Dr. Ed Wilson, who was summoned from a fishing trip on Chesapeake Bay. Then some techniques were applied by Dr. Joseph Peabody, Jr., a great physician to whom I shall always be indebted for literally saving my life. Multiple transfusions of blood were supplied by many beautiful people, known and unknown to me. There were a few comatose periods, some fantastic hallucinations and, believe it or not, a few absurdly comic situations. But after two weeks I walked out of the hospital. Even my departure was not without a humorous sidelight.

Up until the afternoon that I left the hospital, "No visitors" was the order. Of course, that didn't include Jackson, who had planned a visit for the next morning. No one told Jack that I had gone home; so, armed with my room number in order that he wouldn't have to go through the front desk, he showed up at the room—all alone. After a tenuous knock to which there was no response, he entered.

Hospital beds being at a premium, another patient had already been installed. The new man was an octogenarian obviously beset by every common and uncommon ailment known to geriatric medicine. As I was informed later, the poor gentleman had snow-white hair, a skeletal countenance, sunken eyes, and, since he had no teeth, his nose and chin were contiguous. Jackson took one horror-stricken look and screamed, "My God, Frank, what have they done to you?" He was quite certain that the *Harden and Weaver* show would be the *Weaver* show before the day was out. Shortly one of the great staff of nurses at Suburban arrived and assured Jackson that I was alive and well at home. Jack left the octogenarian to his fate and ambled away. But he says he still has visions.

How do you feel—or what do you think of when the idea comes to you that you're about to die? I don't want to get heavy, but I can remember a couple of things that occurred to me at the time.

First, if I felt anything strongly at all, it was not fear at the thought of dying. I was never frightened, or maybe I was afraid but too stupid to recognize it. The one thing I do remember is a feeling of anger. Anger at myself.

"Boy, you've really screwed it up this time. Think of all the things you haven't done. Think of all the places you haven't been. Think of all the experiences you haven't had." I'll be honest and say I didn't dwell on that line of thought too long; I was too busy being apprehensive about what the army of doctors and nurses and attendants were going to do to me next.

Two days after leaving the hospital, I was back on the show. General Manager Andy Ockershausen claims the reason for my rapid recovery was the fact that George Wilson was doing such a good job on the show in my place.

HARDEN AND WEAVER GALLERY

FRANK: Dr. Willoughby, thanks for dropping by. This being the twenty-first day of December, it's the height of the trauma season associated with the Christmas office parties.

WILLOUGHBY: I have more patients than I can handle. I've brought in somebody from Baltimore to help with the caseload. And a young lady came up from Richmond. Now there's no waiting.

FRANK: Is she a parapsychologist or a regular—

WILLOUGHBY: A regular fellow.

FRANK: Now, about the office parties—

WILLOUGHBY: Yes, the thing to remember is they have a terrible residual effect.

FRANK: The Memory Syndrome?

WILLOUGHBY: Yes, an elephant can't hold a candle. Eleven years after the incident while vacationing in New Mexico, your wife will bring it up again. So I suggest you find ways not to attend the party.

FRANK: I understand people are now suing companies because of the company-party shenanigans.

WILLOUGHBY: So remember—it isn't for now—it's forever.

Jackson: Hitting the High Sea

I had never lost my fascination with boats and the sea. All through the years in broadcasting, I still read everything I could get my hands on. Washington was close enough to the Chesapeake Bay and the rivers that feed into it to keep my love for the briny alive. For the first few years during the war, there were no boats being constructed for pleasure—you couldn't even get a car. And then I always seemed to be too busy—spending weekends doing dance band remotes and all the other things. Finally I made my way to the sailing marinas to look the situation over.

My first venture was with a twelve-foot catboat. I had no knowledge of sailing except what I had read. But when you start with a simple boat, you pick things up really fast. I graduated to a twenty-one-foot catboat and sailed that until one day I spotted a Japanese-built sloop on the Maine Avenue waterfront in southwest Washington, and bought it. It was my pride and joy for quite a while. Then I bought a bigger boat, followed by one that I had built. My first five boats were all sailboats. As I became more acquainted with the Chesapeake Bay, I began talking with Jack and Ed Nieman in Shady Side, Maryland. I finally contracted with them to build me a two-masted schooner. This craft ran at around twenty-seven feet. Then my youngsters started growing up and I needed more room. So I had a bugeye built, which is really a skipjack hull. After sailing that baby for quite a while, I decided the time had come to go to power.

I wanted a boat with some personality, but also one where you wouldn't have to fall over the side to know you were on a boat. In an issue of *Rudder* magazine I saw plans for a single-screw, wooden-hulled cruiser. The boat was a trawler type, but it featured a pilothouse and a dummy stack to make it resemble a harbor tug. That was it!

The designer of this boat was Charles Whittholz—a naval architect who happened to live in Silver Spring. I looked him up immediately and told him I was interested in a boat like that, only I needed more space than a thirty-two-footer would provide. Also, having spent more than twenty years on the Chesapeake, I'd come to the conclusion that you need at least forty feet to cover all weather conditions. At my request, Whittholz reworked the plans to make the boat a forty-three-footer, and it was built by Rice Brothers in Reidville, Virginia, along the Rappahannock. I made one oversight. The original design called for a box transom. We later removed the transom and spliced in a handsome rounded stern to complete the tug effect. That's how the *Jack Tar* came along, a source of joy for the Weaver family for many years as we cruise on the Chesapeake and Delaware Bays. The tug's berth is Shady Oaks Marina on West River, Maryland. I've kept my boats there for thirty years—both sail and power—and I wouldn't dare entrust them to anyone but Dick Gunther and his son, Rick.

For my greatest sailing experience, however, I have to thank the U.S. Coast Guard. Harden and Weaver have always cooperated with this organization in its boating safety programs. The commandants and the guardsmen have been friends of ours. Until recent years the Coast Guard was able to concentrate on lifesaving and on education about the perils at sea. Nowadays it has had to become more like a police force—going after drug smugglers or illegal aliens. But several years ago Jim Ward of the Coast Guard called me and asked, "Jack, I know how you like ships. How would you like to spend a week at sea on the bark *Eagle?*" I asked him to repeat the question because it sounded too good to be true. There are only around twelve to fifteen square-riggers on this earth. Just about that time, a memo had come out at the station informing employees that anyone who had worked at WMAL twenty years or more was eligible for an extra week's vacation. Frank hadn't been here twenty years yet, but I had. So I told Frank, "By golly, I'm going to take that extra week and go on that trip aboard the *Eagle.*" That was O.K. by Frank.

When the time came, I packed my sea bag and went to New London, Connecticut, and reported to the captain of the *Eagle.* I was shown my quarters in the officers' section of the stern—way down below near the waterline. It was top of the mark as far as I was concerned. I spent a week aboard this magnificent vessel as a guest of the Coast Guard. We sailed the area between the Grand Banks off Newfoundland and the Cape Cod area. Toward the end of the trip—there were maybe two days left—we put in at Provincetown at the tip of the Cape. The next morning—since it was rough out in the roads—a forty-footer was sent out from shore to pick us up and take us in to Provincetown for a visit. Just getting into the smaller boat was an experience. You had to jump in when the boat was on a rise and then hold on because she dropped like an elevator.

When I got ashore, I decided to call Elsie and tell her where we were and how I was doing. And Elsie informed me that the boss, Andy O., was looking all over for me, that I was supposed to be at work. I told her there must be some mistake, this was my extra week of vacation. But she said that Andy had been trying to contact the ship, but a civilian can't put a call through to an operating Coast Guard ship at sea. I told her it was too late now, anyway, that as far as she was concerned, I hadn't called in.

When the voyage was over, I returned to the station and Andy asked me, "Where have you been?" When I told him, he said it sure sounded like a great trip but I was supposed to be working. I showed him the memo—I had this extra week of vacation. He said of course I was eligible for another week, but the timing had to be subject to discussion. I couldn't just walk out of the building whenever the urge hit me. I guess I was just too excited about the *Eagle* to worry about dotting all those *i*s and crossing all those *t*s.

But it was a little late to worry about it now.

Frank: The Tender(loin) Trap

By some legalistic legerdemain certain crimes have come to be characterized as "victimless." Those terms would seem to be contradictory if not mutually exclusive, but without pretending to understand obscure points of law, I'd like to relate how I believe I became the victim of a "victimless" crime.

One April evening I was delivering a stranded gentleman from a Chevy Chase restaurant to the Madison Hotel. Having done that I found myself alone in my very small sports car in that part of the city known variously as "Streetwalker Strip," "Porno Parade" and other clever euphemisms for the practice of prostitution on public premises. At around 9:30 that night, while I had stopped for a traffic signal at Fourteenth and L streets, one of two females (I can only assume the gender was correct) crossed some thirty feet of sidewalk and approached my car. My vehicle is less than four feet from ground to roof, so this person had to contort herself into a ninety-degree angle even to see inside the car. After assuming this ridiculous posture, she asked if I was "looking for a date." I glanced at the traffic signal to be sure I should still be at a standstill. I was quite aware that by "date" she did not want me to take her to the senior prom. Also during that instant I composed what I thought was a mildly amusing and silly answer to her silly and rude question. I suggested that if she could demonstrate all her arts, crafts and skills right there—before the traffic light changed—it would certainly be worth something to me. May I say that my quick remark received something less than a standing ovation. Before even finishing my bon mot, I was informed through several techniques (barking voices, displays of badges, shining of lights) that I was under arrest. If I had any doubts about that, those doubts were fleeting. In the next moment I was manacled, rudely and roughly tossed into the back of a prowl car, and whisked away to jail.

Again I know nothing of the finer points of law. But since the undercover officer approached me with no invitation, enticement or signal from me, wasn't she soliciting me instead of the reverse? Since the undercover officer started the conversation—making it easy for me to make a remark containing the elements of solicitation—wasn't that entrapment? And could anyone seriously consider what I had said to be true solicitation?

About an hour later my attorney negotiated my release, and I told him my story over coffee at a nearby restaurant. He carefully explained the facts of life about this particular crime—that even if I was entrapped I would first have to admit that I did solicit the lady, but plead that I would not have done so but for her. Great defense.

As if the humiliation and the legal expense were not enough, four days later a television station devoted several minutes to the broadcast of my confrontation with the police. There followed, of course, numerous accounts of the story in the press for days afterward, including one of a subsequent court action. Eight days later *The Washington Post* chose to print this new red-hot news story.

There are those who say that people in the public eye must be ready for such notoriety. But the results of my little remark made to an obviously deceitful person could have brought financial disaster to me and others, professional embarrassment to my employers and serious detractions from my very happy family life. These things did not occur. Instead there was an outpouring of support for me and criticism of police behavior. Hundreds of letters and calls came from friends and strangers. It would seem by this public and private response that the police and the news media came off as the bad guys and the victim as the good guy.

I have been asked the question—and it's a legitimate one—"If you weren't guilty why didn't you fight it?" The answer is obvious. For many and varied considerations which are peculiar to my profession, the less said the better. The option of electing the provisions of the First Offender's Act was simply the most prudent course to end the matter quickly.

I'd still like to know how the behavior of the police officer enhanced the public safety of the community. Judging from the man-hours and paperwork involved in my particular case, the cost of such a program must be huge. I seriously doubt whether the program will eliminate prostitution, reduce crime or enhance the general appearance of the area.

But there is a lesson to be learned. Never make a smartass remark until there has been a complete show of IDs all around. Remarks to the wrong people at the wrong time can be hazardous to your health, happiness, convenience and peace of mind. They can also be expensive. There are times when a one-liner can prove to be remarkably unfunny.

Frank: The Good Old Daze

A while back, I dropped in on my uncle and aunt who live in Coral Gables, Florida. By the way, this uncle, Hollis Calhoun, my departed mother's half brother, is one of the funniest men I have ever known. He just *thinks* funny. His telling the most familiar, mundane family recollection can have me in stitches. He doesn't try to be funny, he doesn't seize opportunities to shoot one-liners, and he doesn't invent funny situations—Hollis just THINKS funny. And he thinks in exaggeration.

One of his first observations upon seeing me on this visit was: "Brother, I'll be damned if this ain't the first time I've seen you when you weren't drunk since you were two years old." Now that was an exaggeration, but it did point up the fact that I had ended a lifetime career of drinking.

You see, I used to drink. Boy, did I drink! Not necessarily in copious quantities, but all the time, man and boy, day and night, year in and year out. It all started quite undramatically and ended equally as undramatically.

There was absolutely no alcohol, not even beer, in my parents' home—ever. My father didn't drink, but he didn't particularly object to others having a nip or two. My mother didn't drink, and, by God, she'd do all she could to keep others from drinking. I can't even remember my first drink, but it must have been consumed sometime when I was fourteen or fifteen years old. From that time until my late fifties, imbibing was more or less a part of my life-style. Sometimes a little once in a while, sometimes none at all for a long period of time, sometimes daily. The pattern wasn't cyclical, and no definitive curves could be plotted showing correlation to this force or that factor or the other pressure in my life. I can honestly say that in all my drinking career I never once approached an event, a holiday, a period of time with "I think I'll go out and hang one on!" As a matter of fact I made it a habit NOT to attend celebrations or go out on New Year's Eve where the norm is to see how pasted one can get. I certainly never drank to bolster my courage, or escape, or drown sorrows, or any of the other clichés so much in currency in the self-analysis pages of the Sunday supplements. My only motivation for drinking was I liked it, I could afford it, and figured my liver was staunch enough to take it.

But what about my professional performance? Did it suffer from a regimen of drinking morning, noon and night? Well, I have performed with a little to drink, after drinking a lot (i.e., drunk), and with a complete absence of drinking; and I am being completely honest when I say that I have turned in good to excellent performances in all three situations. I have also turned in bad to disastrous performances. I don't think one type outnumbers the other in any category. And I'm not saying that in defense of "drinking on the job." Anyone who says his performance is enhanced by a couple of hummers before the show is either stupid or is fooling himself—badly!

While on the subject, I admit that during my driving career, which is roughly coincidental with my drinking career, I have driven long mileage and short mileage in just about every state of sobriety or inebriation known to man. That makes me just about the luckiest man on the face of the earth. I've never been injured or a party to anyone else's injury. But having said that, drunk driving scares the living bejesus out of me! I support any and all laws that would strip a drinker of his driving privileges. Immediate and mandatory revocation of the permit and possibly even incarceration for the drinking driver!

Next question: How and why did you stop drinking? Let me tell you why first. One day during a routine health check, my blood analysis showed some telltale signs of abnormal liver activity. Not cirrhosis, just aberrations in the size of enzymes and stuff like that. Doctor's recommendation? Cut back on alcohol ingestion. How? I thought over that recommendation and came to the conclusion, "Who the hell wants to stop in the middle of the afternoon and count up the number of drinks and beers he's had since six o'clock in the morning? It's a lot easier to cut it out altogether." I'm afraid that's a disappointingly undramatic end to a long and active career of imbibing, but it was as simple as that. I just stopped drinking. Withdrawal pains and anxieties? None. Change in lifestyle? Not particularly. There's still a well-stocked liquor cabinet in my home. There's beer in the fridge. I serve family and friends. As a matter of fact, my name is on the liquor license of a restaurant of which I am part owner. I just decided not to indulge anymore.

I used to be fond of saying, "Sobriety, next to poverty, is the most insufferable state in human existence." I would probably still say it if I thought it would bring a chuckle. But it's not all that bad. Dull, perhaps. Boring most of the time. But not insufferable.

I'm reminded of the time several years ago when, about noon, I found myself "betwixt and between" gigs as it were, with about a half hour or so on my hands. I had just finished some recording at ABC news on Connecticut Avenue, and was due at a film studio in Georgetown in about an hour. So I did the only natural thing to do, I dropped into Duke Zeibert's for a fast shooter. The bar was three deep, as it usually was at Duke's at that time of day, but Mac MacNamara, one of the world's great bartenders, spotted me, knew my choice and handed it to me over a couple of gentlemen seated at the end of the bar. It so happened these gentlemen were discussing something Harden and Weaver had said on the air that morning. They didn't recognize me, and I certainly had no intention of interrupting the conversation.

"You know, I don't know how Harden keeps that show together. Weaver's always half in the bag. Always drunk," observed one authority on the personal lives of the great and near great.

"Yep," said his buddy, thereby reinforcing an already unshakeable truth, "I understand Weaver goes completely bonkers sometimes."

I didn't try to tell them they had the wrong guy. It was amusing though. You can count the number of drinks Jackson has consumed in the last twenty-five years on one hand. I'm in there having a couple of shooters and they're accusing him of being a lush!

Frank: Divorce, Marriage and Other Oft-Told Tales

Somehow I have managed to become a statistic in several diverse categories. Marriages? Two. Divorces? One. Life-threatening episodes? A couple.

Let me tell you about divorce. When it appeared inevitable, I called my attorney, Jimmy Cromwell, and told him of the decision.

"My God, Frank," he said. "Only Rockefellers can afford divorces." And do you know what? That was indeed a wise observation. He was certainly closer to right than wrong. After having invested heavily in the state of Nevada and in the financial well-being of several practitioners of the legal arts in several jurisdictions, I walked away from the situation with the clothes on my back and a Chevrolet automobile. And with two kids in very expensive colleges, and with an outsized alimony obligation staring me in the face, the latter a troublesome condition that has continued until this day.

On one occasion, when I became the defendant in a court action, there was the little matter of serving the necessary papers on me. My attorney told the court he would be happy to accept service of the papers in my behalf, but no, the sheriff's office insisted upon playing Perry Mason. Well, I hardly keep a low profile. I'm on the air four hours a morning, and much of that time is spent in reciting the Harden and

Weaver daily schedule, or in rambling references to where we go and what we do. One day I was at my usual luncheon haunt, Carmack's Restaurant in Chevy Chase, when the hostess said there was a lady in the foyer to see me.

"Bring her in. The more the merrier" was my hail-fellow-well-met response. (Listeners approaching us at lunch were certainly not unheard of. In fact, it was a quite common occurrence.)

Anyway I stood up to greet a young lady who was carrying, of all things, an infant in arms.

"Mr. Harden?," she ventured. "Yes" was my scintillating response. She reached into the back of the baby's diaper and unfurled an official-looking document—albeit a bit soggy. And that was the rather unusual way I was served papers to appear in court. I understand sheriffs' offices engage paid process servers to devise clever ruses to do their jobs. All this seemed so unnecessary, when all it took was a telephone call to arrange a time and a place.

But ho-hum, the alimony continues. Am I bitter? Not really. Suicidal at times perhaps, but not bitter.

I am now very happily married and have been for about twelve years. And that happiness has generated an unusual phenomenon. I don't feel twelve years older than when Berit and I were married, I feel at least twenty years younger!

"Berit is a strange name," you say. The name is not necessarily strange where she comes from, which is northern Sweden—Tanaby, to be exact. A beautiful part of the world, just below the Arctic Circle. I've visited Tanaby many times, and I always say this about the Arctic Circle: "If you've seen one, you've seen 'em all."

We both enjoy reading and traveling, and when it comes to reading fare, Berit gives me a decided inferiority complex. Though I read a lot (usually best-sellers), she consumes

French classics—in French. And that's only one of the languages she's fluent in. Others are Swedish, German, English, and now, by God, she has taken up Chinese with heavy graduate school courses. When I try my high school Spanish on the maid, all I get is giggles. Well, I never could learn to ice skate or win at pinball either.

I have two sons. The oldest, Bob—a Brown University graduate—is in financial management and lives in Oxnard Shores, California. My daughter, Daphne, received her degree in behavioral sciences from Case Western Reserve University; I'm not sure of the connection, but she is involved in fashion design in New York. My youngest son, Jeff, studied design and other art-related subjects at the University of Denver. He is now in New York, where he is engaged in "rehabbing" loft space into living quarters and in other speculative ventures.

HARDEN AND WEAVER GALLERY

FRANK:	Yes. Come in, Bosco Osgood.
BOSCO (on phone):	Bosco Osgood here at present time.
FRANK:	We didn't expect to hear from you today. What are you reporting on this morning?
BOSCO:	A thing of great interest. People lining up to get tickets to the Redskins' game.
FRANK:	I hate to bring this up, Bosco, but all the tickets are gone.
BOSCO:	I'm in line right now and I don't think it looks bad at all. Everybody's been talking about the long lines—but I don't see—

FRANK: Bosco, the tickets are all gone—

BOSCO: I'm first in line and nobody else is here. As soon as they open the office, I'll get the tickets. I'm standing at the door of the Capital Centre.

FRANK: Capital Centre—Bosco they sold the tickets at RFK Stadium.

BOSCO: Hello.

(Dial tone)

Jackson: "On the Serious Side"

Religion has come to play an important part in my life, but it wasn't always that way. When I was very small, I believe my folks were Methodists, but I never went to church and I didn't know what it was all about. But in 1935 something happened that was to chart a course for the Weaver family.

My father worked nights, and he was returning home early one morning, walking along the street, when a booklet sticking out of a trashcan caught his eye. Across the top the booklet read: 'Millions Now Living Will Never Die!' He picked it out of the trash, dusted it off and took it home. He tossed it on the kitchen table and said to my mother, "Here's something I thought you might find interesting." She picked it up and eventually read it clear through. That's how my mother became interested in Jehovah's Witnesses. Our association with the Witnesses began soon after that, and it wasn't long before we all became Jehovah's Witnesses—all, ironically, except my father, who had touched off the whole thing in the first place.

My active association with the Buffalo congregation of Jehovah's Witnesses continued all through my school years. With other members of my family, I regularly called at the homes of neighbors to carry the message. My father had no objections to the family's hosting a weekly study of the Bible in our home. When I was seventeen I dedicated my life to the service of Jehovah God, and symbolized my spiritual resolve by being baptized.

When I was eighteen and left for the radio announcing job in Manitowoc, Wisconsin, I was leaving home for the first time. I also left my active association with Jehovah's Witnesses. I became engrossed in broadcasting and there didn't seem to be enough time for anything else. The principles I'd been taught earlier were still within me. It was always my intent to become active again. But in spite of all those good intentions, it was nearly five years before I was again actively involved with Jehovah's Witnesses. In the meantime I had married Elsie and we had our three sons.

One day in 1953 an elderly lady came to our house as part of her regular activity of ministering for the Witnesses from house to house. She spoke first to Elsie, and what she said was strongly reminiscent of the things I had told my wife about my early religious experiences. The woman was named Sister Hilgers, and she started to call regularly on my wife. Elsie liked what she was hearing, even though it was vastly different from her own religious upbringing. As a consequence she encouraged Sister Hilgers to come back at a time when I would be home so she could talk with me. She did and I responded favorably. When she returned the following week, she brought a couple with her—Charles and Verdie Eberly—who then started a regular weekly study of the Bible with us in our home. I credit that home Bible study with reawakening my spiritual side. I became active again and began attending meetings regularly at the Ashton, Maryland, Kingdom Hall.

Because I had been away from the Witnesses for such a long time, and because I came to feel I had not completely understood my earlier dedication, I was baptized a second time in 1956, along with Elsie. We have continued our active association with the organization. Our sons were all very young, and the Bible became like Dr. Spock in our house.

I set out to become what I consider to be the complete

spiritual man. The requirements were right there in the Bible. They included moral conduct, orderliness, reasonableness and the ability to teach the Bible's important principles. They are characteristics that make an impact on all aspects of a person's life. More than just indulging in an intellectual exercise, you have to exert yourself vigorously to demonstrate a balanced and healthful outlook toward relationships within your own family and in the congregational family.

In the late 1950s I became an appointed servant in the Silver Spring, Maryland, congregation of Jehovah's Witnesses. As a servant, I was called upon to take the lead in conducting our public meetings, and I provided counsel and assistance on a personal level wherever it was needed.

My religious life and my career in radio and television sometimes collided in a classic mixture of fantasy and reality. I was doing the Uncle Flapjack children's show at the time, and my character had become very well known to most kids. Our work as Jehovah's Witnesses takes us to the homes of people in our neighborhood. So as I walked through the streets, kids would recognize me as Uncle Flapjack and flock around me shouting my name. Sometimes it was difficult to discuss a serious Bible theme amid the pandemonium caused by my public image.

On other occasions, people would be a little startled when they opened their doors and found Jackson Weaver standing there. They weren't sure I wasn't there to deliver some radio-station-contest prize. It wasn't always easy to focus their attention on the real reason for my call.

My present congregation is in Ashton and the Kingdom Hall, as we call our meeting places, was built by the Witnesses themselves. Elsie and I worked alongside the other members of the congregation during the construction. It was a very satisfying time . . . with men and women of all races, young and old, representing all economic classes, watching our Kingdom Hall come to life.

Frank: Dotting the *T*s and Crossing the *I*s

We've always had a good relationship with the radio station management. After all, it was management that provided us with the opportunity to do the show. They could have chosen someone else for it, and perhaps the program would have been just as successful. I like to think it wouldn't have been—but who knows?

People ask us how come we have to work on Saturdays, making it a six-day-week *Harden and Weaver* program. There was a time when radio ignored the weekends—they weren't considered very saleable, and it was believed that people had other things to do than listen to the radio. Then one day in the 1950s over at the NBC radio network, Pat Weaver launched a show called *Monitor*, and it revolutionized forever the industry's thinking about weekends. It was a most successful magazine concept of news, information and entertainment, and it made weekend radio a real force in broadcasting.

So it was decided at the outset that the *Harden and Weaver* program would run six days. Bill Malone—who had preceded us—also was on the air six days, but he always recorded the Saturday show on Friday. We were given that option, but it never appealed to us. In fact, we found the whole idea unsatisfactory. The success of our show depends on its spontaneity—the ability to react to whatever is happening—the ability to be topical. Besides, it was a tremendous hassle trying to record such a long show on Thursdays or Fridays—what came out on tape just wasn't worth all the trouble. So we decided to come in and do the thing live. We did work a deal whereby we'd get a certain number of Saturdays off. But we received a great many complaints from people. Their arguments went this way: "We get to listen to Harden and Weaver for only about fifteen or twenty minutes each morning before we go to work. Then on Saturdays when we could listen to you for much longer periods of time, you take off." That bothered us enough so that around five years ago we decided to work every Saturday. It would be nice to have two days off a week, but people seem to depend on us as if we're some kind of public utility. When they turn on WMAL in the morning, they expect us to be there—just like the electric lights when they hit the switch. We won't argue with that kind of loyalty.

Getting back to our relationship with management, it's always been mutually accommodating. We've never gone in and pounded the table and made demands. It's not our style to play the role of petulant, tempestuous talent. We don't even have an agent. Many people in our price range—and many who make a lot less—engage agents to do their bargaining for them. Some people despair of the fact that we *don't* have representation. They tell us we are missing the boat, that we could get a lot more money, that the way we do business is old-fashioned and we should wise up. Maybe so.

We go in and have a friendly conversation with management and come out with what we think is fair and what they apparently think is fair. It's as simple as that. We've never been holdouts. We've never become "free agents." And that's the way we've operated from the very first contract.

However, in this framework there's a certain protocol, a pecking order, that lays out who is in charge of what. So when contract time comes around, there's always junior number one or junior number two who comes along and says negotiating the Harden and Weaver contract is his responsibility. Well, the fact is we've already had our chat with top management and settled the contract. But top management requests that we play this little charade and go through the motions of contract settlement. We have a big talk with junior number one or two, but it means absolutely nothing. We realize there are certain people who have to feel they are in on the big decisions—so we play the game. It's all a bit silly, but there's no harm done.

However, we are dealing with enlightened management. We do the program and they take care of the rest. I don't think I've ever seen the station's rate card. When we go out socially and meet other people in the trade, they mention our ratings and our rate card, and they might as well be talking about nuclear fission as far as I'm concerned. Unless we happen upon it by accident, we don't know all those things—no one encumbers us with them. Maybe by not making ourselves privy to that information, we are fools—but I doubt that seriously. I know one thing. I would never be one to make some kind of a deal for a percentage of the gross—or a "per spot" arrangement. I like the sure thing. I prefer to know that if the economic picture takes a sudden downward turn, I'm still getting the same salary. It's pay or play for me.

HARDEN AND WEAVER GALLERY

FRANK: Larry, I understand after all these years they are going to take your program off the air. Does it have something to do with violence?

LARRY: Absolutely not. I can honestly say there has never been any violence on our program. We've had saxophones and drums, but never any violence.

Frank: The Two of Us

What if there had been no *Harden and Weaver* show? Where would I be now, and what would I be doing? I try not to think about that too much. When Harden and Weaver got under way, I was doing all right. There were very few announcers who could point to two sponsored network programs, so I was more than comfortable. But the day of the staff announcer was almost over—we were definitely an endangered species by the time the 1960s came along. In their latest agreements with the unions, the networks have abandoned the staff-announcer concept. They have attrition clauses in the contract—those who have the jobs will have them for life, but no announcers are being replaced. It's the end of the line. There have been "buy-outs"—paying the announcer a sum of money to retire.

There was a time when a staff announcer and only a staff announcer could perform certain duties—like system cues and introductions to news programs—but that's all history. I guess that unless I was the beneficiary of a grandfather clause, I would have gone the way of all staff announcers. I'm not even sure I would have remained in the radio business.

Probably the question most frequently asked us has to do with our personal relationship. First of all, I can answer that there's no master plan or covenant of any kind between us. We never sat down and made a list of dos and don'ts. We

never delineated responsibilities or drew up a code of conduct or any kind of informal arrangement. Our interaction is completely natural, and I believe our relationship—after some thirty-odd years—is based on honesty, mutual respect and a complete absence of anything synthetic. There is no "showbiz" hype as far as we are concerned.

When disagreements occur—and of course they do—there is no need for confrontation. First of all, confrontation is uncomfortable for both of us; and second, the tension of such a situation would surely be apparent in our air performance. We both have philosophies and differences that are not that important. In politics I am a social liberal (though a fiscal conservative), and though Jackson has never made any formal pronouncement on the subject, I suspect he is of a more conservative political stripe.

Religion is a subject that can open a chasm in a relationship if anything can. I know we are poles apart on that subject. But we have never indulged in any personal religious or philosophical dialogues. Of course, I have heard Jackson announce and discuss his views and beliefs many times, and he has heard mine. I can find no more concord with his views than he can with mine. But none of that has anything to do with our team mission of putting on an acceptable radio program. Jackson is allied with and quite active in the Jehovah's Witnesses movement. However, he has never tried in any way to convert me into a communicant. The fact that I cannot intellectually accept any anthropomorphic concept of a deity has not alienated Jackson. Nor do I go around preaching to others what I consider to be the error of their mystic ways. We are both acutely aware of this basic difference in our attitudes toward things spiritual, but that difference has never been an agent to adulterate the Harden and Weaver chemical formula.

We see very little of each other outside our professional

duties. We didn't consciously decide to do that—it just happened. At ten o'clock in the morning he goes his way and I go mine; he has his circle of friends and his interests, and I have mine, and they seldom intersect. He's owned boats all of his adult life—at least ever since I've known him—and I think I've been aboard his craft only two or three times. He's never stayed at my house at the beach—though he would be most welcome.

The focus of our common activity is not apt to be Colesville, Maryland, where Jackson lives. It's more likely to be Chevy Chase or the District of Columbia, where I operate—so he probably knows more of my friends than I know of his. If the civic clubs or professional groups or other organizations where we speak had their activities in Colesville, then the reverse would be true.

We are completely different personalities, even though we've been together so long we tend to think alike or to anticipate alike. For example, if a conversation is going on, we're apt to have the same observation and come up with the same response or at least the same reaction. Sometimes it's actually spooky! I'm about to say something and Jackson pops out with it first, and it happens the other way around. I guess it's simply the result of so many shared experiences.

As for Jackson's talent, I am forever awed by it. I don't know how he does it, but he can effortlessly go in and out of one voice after another with flawless syntax. He'll use the first person in one particular voice and then switch to another voice. Everything always comes out just exactly right. And he does it *naturally*. There are only rare instances when I have tried to lead him into a certain character and he has come up with the wrong one. When that occurs, it is smoothed over easily. I've accused Jackson of being a multischizophrenic—he can identify with all those imaginary people, he gets deep down into their characters. Now, Jonathan Winters has no peer in doing that sort of thing—but he's looking through a different window at his people, an advantage that Jackson doesn't have. His characters are all superimposed on a single, very normal basic one.

Some people—schoolteachers among them—have taken issue with some of Jackson's grammar. The fact is, Jackson uses the idiom to communicate and is far more successful than most communicators. He has an uncanny ability to impart an idea—whether the idea is original or whether he is transmitting the thoughts of others. His misuse of acceptable grammatical formulas does not interfere one iota with his ability to communicate. As a matter of fact, whether Jackson is imparting a thought that is serious, clever, amusing or downright absurd, I suggest that the impact on one's perception is more effective than that of, say, a Peter Ustinov or an Alistair Cooke—with all their impeccable usage. Many times I know I am guilty of driving a simple thought straight into confusion in my effort to turn a clever phrase.

At the end of a William Buckley pronouncement, you might be moved to ask, "What did he say?" But when Jackson speaks, you are completely satisfied that you not only know what he said, but probably understood every word, every syllable, every meaning, every *shade* of meaning and every subtlety. Who would you say is the more effective communicator?

Jackson: The Two of Us

What amazes me is that Frank has been able to put up with me all these years. It proves that he is a patient man. Frank brings things to the show that are out of my realm. He's the intellectual—the one with a storehouse of information. He can consume and retain things to the point where he's like an encyclopedia. I have nothing but admiration for his ability to recall almost everything. Frank's like the WMAL Answer Man—you ask a question and he says, "Oh, I know exactly what you're talking about." And he does.

We've been working side by side at the same table for twenty-two years, and I can't remember our ever having a flare-up. Maybe the fact that Frank and I rarely see each other socially helps. On the job after all these years, there is a flow, a rhythm that we achieve without even trying. I can get up in the middle of the show, be gone for ten minutes and nothing is really interrupted. He can do the same thing. We have no surprises for each other.

Everything we've ever done has been on an equal basis. Each of us will always refer to "Harden and Weaver"—never to "my show." We know how important we are to each other. When one person is sick and can't work, the other one takes the day off. There's no sense trying to work with someone else, and working alone is just not the same.

I don't know what I'd be doing now if there had been no *Harden and Weaver* show. I was very much caught up in acting in the early days—perhaps I would have tried my luck as a character actor on the stage in New York or on some television situation comedy. But I would have been hard pressed to leave the Washington area. I found it a good place to raise my family, and the Chesapeake Bay was near enough to satisfy all my urges to go to sea. The older you get, the more you realize that becoming a big star performer isn't so important. I have my ego massaged enough right here.

One on Two

ED: Have you changed much in your approach to your work since the early days?

FRANK: I suppose anyone would get a little jaded after a while. There was a time when I listened to tapes—listened to what other people were doing. I don't do that anymore. I still have pride in what I do, but I'm not like an actor on the stage who still expects to soar to dizzying heights by performing the ultimate role. I think I've soared about as high as I'm going to soar, and as often as I have played it, this role is always exciting—always new.

ED: Is it difficult to stay fresh?

JACKSON: This may sound like a cop-out, but I don't think our listeners expect us to be too fresh. Most of our routine is built on repetition. Jack Benny was the ultimate master at that.

FRANK: I suppose there are people who wake up in the morning who dread going to work. I look forward to it. I think if there comes a day when I no longer feel that way it will be time to retire.

ED: Do you still have the same affection for the place where you work as you did in the old days?

FRANK: Let me tell you something about that. I'll never forget one time—before Harden and Weaver—when AFTRA was negotiating a new contract. This was in the days when the station was in the doldrums. I was sitting in on the negotiations—as most AFTRA members did—and one of the management team began making some petty demands about work rules, and I said, "You're talking bush league—this is WMAL." And he looked at me and said, "Frank, I've got news for you—WMAL *is* bush league!" That hurt me. I never considered the station bush league. I saw it as a five-thousand-watt station in a major market with a prestigious past and a lot of potential.

JACKSON: A radio station is just a lot of electronic equipment. It's the people who give a station its fiber—its personality. A young announcer has a tendency to jump around trying to better himself. But WMAL is the only place where I never had itchy feet. We feel we *are* WMAL—the people you hear on the air are the listeners' conception of the station.

FRANK: One time the broadcast executives got together to start what they called the Broadcasters' Club. They began thinking about credentials for membership, and one of the organizers said, "Now this is going to be a real broadcasters' club—we don't want any of those clowns who are on the air." His conception of a broadcaster was the executive, the one who controls the business. I suppose that's one way of looking at it.

ED: Do you notice a difference in the approach of young people looking for work now over what it was years ago?

JACKSON: There seems to be a reluctance to go out into the boondocks. Everybody wants to start right out in a major market—looking for what they now call "entry-level" jobs. The small station is still an excellent place to learn a great many things about how the business works. You don't get stuck in one department—never really knowing what most of the people in the station are doing.

FRANK: Young people also seem less eager to do things just to get the exposure—work the bad shifts, put in the long hours, give up the social life—concentrating on building a career. But I must say there are more bright, aware young people coming into the business now than ever before.

Jackson: I See by the Old Clock on the Wall

Young people often ask us how to go about preparing for a career in broadcasting, and the question is a real stumper. When you talk about performing, you're dealing with something that's very hard to define. People don't even agree on which performers they like best. I hate to admit this but there are people out there who can't stand Harden and Weaver. The audience makes the judgment, and unlike the stage, the radio audience is a ghost. There is no immediate bounce back. There are performers who need a live audience—to stimulate them, to bring their performances up. In radio somehow you have to build a rapport with that unseen audience. Some people can never do it. Certain people can and then suddenly lose the ability. Some people can go on having that rapport as long as they live. And no one's quite sure why.

So how do you go about becoming a performer? There are two schools of thought. One puts the emphasis on mechanics—voice, diction and so forth. The other emphasizes communicating ideas regardless of skills. Good performers have come from both schools. So have bad performers.

A true professional can probably talk with you for ten or fifteen minutes and be able to tell you whether you would be better off in some other line of work. There are certain speech or voice-quality problems that are almost impossible to overcome. But some vocational schools will always represent themselves as being able to teach you how to become an accomplished performer. They'll take your tuition money no matter how hopeless your prospects may be, and they'll tell you that you've got what it takes.

To those who are serious about entering the business, we *do* recommend the communications departments of various universities. You will learn many of the fundamentals and become familiar with the equipment; and you will discover rather quickly where your strengths and weaknesses are. For example, you may come to the conclusion that you prefer management, or programming, or engineering. Most universities have campus radio stations where you will get the opportunity to try out your skills.

At the same time, we have to admit that we had no such preparation when we broke into the business. There were no communications departments in the universities in the early days.

Again, let me say there are certain elements of performing that are not teachable. What you are really looking for is a quality that makes you click with an audience without trying to—or at least not noticeably trying. What is it? I don't know. It's a gift. Another question we get a lot is "What does your job entail—what really is it that you do?" That's another toughie. So we tell a little story—a parable that we feel may provide a satisfactory answer. Here it is:

THE STORY TAKES PLACE IN WEST VIRGINIA, WHERE WE FIND A MAN WALKING DOWN A COUNTRY ROAD WITH A LIVE PIG UNDER ONE ARM, A LIVE CHICKEN UNDER THE OTHER ARM AND A WASHTUB BALANCED ON HIS HEAD. THE MAN IS OBVIOUSLY lost, and when he spots a house, he goes up to it to see if he can get some directions. Encumbered as he is, the man kicks at the door and a lady appears. "Ma'am," he says, "I wonder if you could direct me to the Snyder residence?" And the lady looks him over for a minute and says finally, "Well, I guess I could. Tell you what you do. You go on down there to the dry crick bed—you follow that about five hundred yards until you come to a big stump—what's left of a tree that was hit by lightnin' in 1947. At that point, you start on up the hill to the southeast and . . ."

"Hold up, ma'am," he says. "You're talking to probably the worst person in the world when it comes to takin' directions. I'll get lost for sure. I wonder if your kindness would extend to accompanying me to the foot of that hill and then pointing me in the right direction?" The lady took on a rather skeptical look and said, "Well, you must think I'm addled."

"Why do you say that?" asked the man.

"Because you could get me down there and then take advantage of me."

The man could hardly believe what he had heard. "Ma'am," he said, "you can see I got a pig under one arm, a chicken under the other and this washtub on my head. How could I do anything like what you say?"

"Oh, I know what you'd do," said the lady. "You'd just upend that tub and put the pig under it, that's what!"

"YES," SAID THE MAN, "BUT WHAT ABOUT THE CHICKEN?"

AND THE LADY QUICKLY REPLIED, "OH, I'D HOLD THAT FER YA!"

And that, my friends, is exactly what Harden and Weaver do. Every morning, we hold your chicken for you.

Index